TRUE DEVOTION
TO MARY

by

ST. LOUIS MARY DE MONTFORT

Translated from the original French by
FRANÇOISE DE CASTRO, Ph.D., T.O.P.

Adapted by
EDDIE DOHERTY, T.O.P.

MONTFORT PUBLICATIONS

Imprimi Potest:
    FRANK A. SETZER, S.M.M.,
                        Provincial Superior.

Nihil Obstat:
    MARTINUS S. RUSHFORD, PH.D.,
                        Censor Librorum.

Imprimatur:
    ✠ THOMAS EDMUNDUS MOLLOY, S.T.D.,
          Archiepiscopus-Episcopus Bruklyniensis.

Bruklyni, die XXVI April 1956.

6th Printing—2002

ISBN 0-910984-02-6

ST. LOUIS DE MONTFORT
(St. Peter's, Rome)

FOREWORD

EVER since its discovery, in 1842, St. Louis De Montfort s treatise on True Devotion to Mary has been a best-seller in the Catholic Church. Rarely has one book been the butt of so much abuse; rarely has one book received so many papal commendations! Translated into some forty or more languages, its popularity far from decreasing has increased with the years, particularly with the advent of the Marian age in which we now live.

From the first English translation, by the well-known English writer, Father Frederick William Faber, down to our own latest American editions, there has been a constant concern on the part of the editors to adapt De Montfort's style and terminology to the contemporary modes of expression, without in any way watering down the doctrine or misrepresenting the author's thought.

Despite these attempts, however, some still find the book difficult to understand. Some of the Saint's words and expressions, although theologically accurate, are sometimes misunderstood. Hence, the need for a broader translation, one that will express the saintly author's thought in different words and in a style that is popular and easily understood by the average layman.

For such a difficult task one could hardly be better qualified than Eddie Doherty, one of America's finest and most popular Catholic writers, editor, reporter and Slave of Jesus and Mary. Undertaken at our request, Mr. Doherty has made of this a work of love. With the help of Miss Francoise de Castro, Ph.D., who gave him a word-for-word translation from the original French, the writer made the adaptation you now hold in your hands.

Although the student of Mariology and those concerned with getting De Montfort's thought, as expressed in the original manuscript, will prefer the standard edition, we feel that Eddie Doherty's version will open the way to many other souls by whom De Montfort's treatise might otherwise have remained unexplored. We hope that its fresh, breezy style will lead many more souls to a better understanding of the De Montfort way of life.

THE EDITORS.

CHAPTER I

REIGN OF CHRIST THROUGH MARY

THROUGH the Immaculate Virgin Mary, Jesus Christ came into the world. Through her He will reign over the world.

Mary lived in obscurity during most of her life. Her humility was so great that she desired to hide, not only from all other creatures, but even from herself, so that only God should know her. She asked Him to conceal her, and to make her poor and humble. God delighted to hide her; in her conception, in her birth, in her mysteries, in her resurrection and assumption.

Her own parents did not know her. And the angels asked "Who is she?" The Most High, though He revealed something of her perfection to the angels, kept infinitely more from them.

God the Father willed she should work no miracle—at least no striking one—in her life. Yet He had given her the power to work tremendous miracles.

God the Son was content she should speak but a few words. Yet He had endowed her with His wisdom.

And God the Holy Ghost arranged that His apostles and evangelists should say little about her—no more than enough to make Christ known. Yet she was His beloved spouse.

Mary is God's masterpiece whose full splendor He has reserved for Himself.

She is the admirable Mother of the divine Son, Who took delight in humbling and hiding her to favor her sweet humility. He called her "woman," as though she were a stranger; yet she was dearer to Him than all men and angels.

She is the sealed fountain, the faithful spouse of the Holy Ghost. She is the sanctuary, the resting place of the Trinity. God dwells in her more wonderfully, more divinely, than anywhere else in the universe, including the regions occupied by the angelic hosts. And no creature, however pure, is admitted to that sanctuary except through a great privilege.

With all the saints I say that our Mother Mary is the paradise on earth where the new Adam took flesh, through the operation of the Holy Ghost, that He might work there wonders beyond all understanding. She is the great, the divine world of God where lie beauties and treasures one cannot imagine. She is the magnificence of God!

What grand and secret things God has worked in her. Even she must admit it. "He that is mighty hath done great things to me." The world does not know these wonders. It is unworthy of knowing them. It is incapable of understanding them.

The saints have said many beautiful things about Mary, the holy city of God; and never were they more eloquent than when they spoke of her. Yet they realized that the heights of her merits could not be glimpsed; for they reach up to the throne of God. They knew that the width of her charity could not be measured, since it is broader than the earth. They know that there were no limits to her power, because she has power over God Himself. They knew that the depths of her humility—and of all her other virtues and graces— could never be fathomed.

O height beyond our understanding! O width beyond all words! O greatness beyond all measures! O depth beyond all human thought or comprehension!

Every day, throughout the world, in the highest heavens, and in the lowest pits of hell, all things proclaim and preach the wonders of the Virgin-Mother.

The nine choirs of angels, the people on earth—even the devils themselves—have to call her Blessed. So great is the power of truth.

The angels in heaven, according to St. Bonaventure, never stop calling to her, "Holy, holy, holy Mary, Virgin Mother of God!" A million times a day they give her the angelic greeting, "Hail Mary!" They prostrate themselves before her. They beg her to honor them with her commands. St. Michael, the prince of the heavenly court, is the most eager to pay her homage, St. Augustine says, and to run her errands.

The whole earth is filled with her glory. Cities, provinces, dioceses, and great nations are placed, by Christians, under her care and protection. Cathedrals are dedicated to God in her name. There is no church without an altar in her honor. There is no district or country without some miraculous image of her; without some place in which she heals all kinds of ills, in which she distributes all sorts of blessings. There are countless organizations that honor her. There are many religious orders sharing her name and her motherly love. Religious men and women constantly sing her praises and proclaim her mercies. Little children just learning the Hail Mary praise and love her. Even the most hardened sinners have some spark of confidence in her.

And yet, with the saints, we must truthfully confess that "There is never enough about Mary." We have not given her enough praise, glory, honor, love, or service. She deserves much more honor from us, greater admiration, better service, and far more love.

Earth vies with heaven to glorify her. Yet we must say with the Holy Ghost, "All the glory of the King's daughter is within." The glory given her by angels and men is as nothing compared to that which she receives from her Maker. This glory the little creatures do not know. Who can penetrate the secret of secrets of the King?

The eye has not seen, the ear has not heard, nor has the heart of man known the beauty, the treasures, and the wonders of Mary. She is the miracle of miracles of grace, of nature, and of glory. She is the worthy Mother of God. If you want to understand the Mother, try to understand the Son.

Let all tongues be silent here!

My heart dictated these words. I wrote them with a special joy to show that our most holy Mary still remains unknown. This is partly the reason why we do not know Jesus Christ as we should. He will be known, of course; and His kingdom will come. This is certain. But this will happen only after the Blessed Virgin is known, and has begun to reign.

She gave Him birth the first time. She will bring Him forth when He comes to us again.

CHAPTER II

NECESSARY TO GOD

MARY, made by the hands of the Most High, is, we all acknowledge, merely a creature. Compared with God's infinite majesty she is less than an atom. We might say she is as nothing. God alone is "He Who Is." He does not depend on anyone. He is sufficient unto Himself. He did not, and still does not, have any absolute need of Mary to accomplish His will and to manifest His glory. To do all things, He has only to will them. But He did will to begin and end His greatest works through her. We may well believe He will not change. He is God and does not change either His sentiments or His conduct.

FOR THE INCARNATION

It was through her, God gave His only begotten Son to the world. For thousands of years the patriarchs sighed and the prophets and holy men begged for this Treasure; but it was only Mary who was worthy to receive Him. She found grace before God by the power of her prayers and the fragrance of her virtues.

The world was unworthy of receiving the Son directly from the Father, St. Augustine tells us. Therefore the Father ordained that Christ, His Son, should be given to the world by Mary.

Christ became man for our salvation. He did so in Mary and through Mary.

God the Holy Ghost formed Christ in Mary; after He had sent one of heaven's foremost ambassadors to win her full consent.

God the Father imparted His fruitfulness to Mary, in such measure as a mere creature could receive it. Thus He gave her the power to produce His divine Son, and also all the members of His Mystical Body.

God the Son entered Mary's virginal womb, as the new Adam in His earthly paradise. In her He was well pleased. In her He worked secret wonders of grace.

God, made man, found His freedom by imprisoning Himself in her womb! He revealed His power by allowing Himself to be carried by a little girl! He found His glory, and that of His Father, by hiding it from all earthly creatures, Mary excepted. He glorified His independence and His majesty by willing to depend upon her at His conception, at His birth, at His presentation in the Temple, and in His hidden years. He willed she should be present at His death, so that He might make but one same sacrifice with her, and with her consent be immolated to the Eternal Father—as Isaac was offered as a sacrifice, with Abraham's consent—to the will of God.

She nursed Him, fed Him, attended Him, brought Him up. And she sacrificed Him for us!

O wonderful and awesome dependence of Almighty God!

Although in the Gospels the Holy Ghost has revealed but few of the marvelous things the Incarnate Wisdom accomplished during His hidden life, He could not keep this dependence secret. He let it be known so that we might see its infinite value.

Jesus gave more glory to His Father by submitting to His Mother for thirty years than He would have given Him by working the greatest miracles and converting the whole world!

What great glory we give God when, to please Him and to imitate Jesus, our supreme Model, we too submit to Mary!

Christ willed to begin His miracles by Mary. He sanctified John the Baptist in the womb of Elizabeth through the words of Mary. No sooner had she spoken than the unborn babe was made holy. This is the first miracle of grace, and the greatest He performed. At the wedding in Cana He listened to Mary's humble prayer, and changed water into wine. This is the first miracle of nature Jesus worked.

He began to work miracles through Mary. He continues to work them through her. And He will go on working them through her until the end of time.

God the Holy Ghost is barren in God. That is, no other Divine Person proceeds from Him. He became fruitful by Mary whom He espoused. It is with her, in her, and of her, that He brought forth Christ, His Masterpiece. And it is with her, in her, and of her that He brings forth, daily, His chosen ones, the members of the Mystical Body, of which Christ is the adored Head.

Therefore the more clearly He sees Mary, His dear inseparable spouse, living in a soul, the more mightily He works to bring forth Jesus in that soul, and that soul in Jesus!

We do not mean to say that the Blessed Virgin makes the Holy Ghost fruitful. Being God, He is, equally with the Father and the Son, infinitely fruitful. What I want to say is that the Holy Ghost deigns to use the Blessed Virgin to produce His fruits—though, absolutely speaking, He does not need to do so. He brings forth in her and through her, Jesus Christ and His members. This is a mystery of grace. Even the most learned, the most spiritual Christians do not understand it.

FOR MAN'S SANCTIFICATION

Such was the method of operation used by the three Persons of the Blessed Trinity in the Incarnation and first coming of Jesus Christ. They still work in this way, every day, invisibly, in the Holy Church; and They will continue to do so until time ends in the second coming of Christ.

God the Father gathered all the waters together and called it the sea. (The Latin word for sea is *Mare.*) He gathered all His graces together and called it Mary. (The Latin is *Maria.*) He has a treasury, a storehouse full of riches. There He has enclosed all He holds most beautiful, striking, rare, and precious, including His own Son. This immense treasury is none but Mary. The saints called her the "treasury of God." From the fullness of this treasury all are made rich!

God the Son imparted to His Mother all the infinite merits and virtues He acquired through His life and death. He made her the treasurer of all the riches He inherited from His Father. Through her He showers on the members of His Mystical Body all His merits, graces, and virtues. She is the mysterious channel, the gentle and generous stream, the gracious aqueduct through which His mercies flow.

God the Holy Ghost enriched His faithful spouse with gifts undreamed of. And He selected her to distribute all that is His, as she wills, when she wills, as much as she wills, to whom she wills. No heavenly gift comes to earth that does not pass through her virginal hands. This is the will of God; that whatever we receive we receive through Mary.

Thus does the Trinity enrich, elevate, and honor her who made herself poor, humble, and hidden; who reduced herself into nothingness through her profound humility.

These are the sentiments of the Church and the Holy Fathers of the Church.

If I should confront the proud thinkers of this century I would bring further proof of all I state here so simply. I would bring in passages from the Holy Scriptures, and quotations from the Fathers of the Church. I would give many sound and logical arguments. But I speak for the poor and simple, who, because they have good will and more faith than most scholars, better understand the truth.

Grace perfects nature, and glory perfects grace. It is certain therefore that Our Lord is as much the Son of Mary, now in heaven, as He was on earth. He has retained the submission of the most perfect of children toward the best of mothers.

Let us be careful here. Let us not suppose that dependence on Mary abases Jesus Christ, or that it is due to any imperfection in Him. Mary is infinitely below her Son. He is God. She does not give orders to Him, as earthly mothers do to their children. Mary is completely transformed in God, by the grace and glory that transforms the holy. Hence she never asks, wills, or does anything contrary to the eternal changeless will of God.

When the saints tell us that all things in heaven and on earth, including God Himself, are subjected to the Blessed Virgin, they mean that the authority God gave her is so great that she appears to have the same power as the Trinity, and that her prayers and requests have such an effect upon God that He receives them as commands. He never denies the prayer of His dear Mother, because she is always humble and conformed to His will.

Moses, by the strength of his prayer, appeased God's anger against the Israelites. That prayer was so powerful the

Lord Most High, the Lord Infinitely Merciful, could not resist it. He asked Moses to let Him be angry and punish this
rebellious people. But the humble prophet prevailed. What,
then, must we think of the prayer of the worthy mother of
God? Is it not more powerful over Infinite Power than all
the prayers of the angels and saints in heaven and on earth?

Mary rules over the angels and the blessed in heaven.
God, to reward her humility, has empowered and commis-
sioned her to put saints on the thrones vacated by the angels
who fell through pride. The Most High, Who exalts the
humble, has willed it so. The lowly virgin He has made queen
of heaven and earth so heaven and earth—and willy-nilly, hell
itself—must bend to her commands.

Mary is the head of God's troops, the treasurer of His
treasures, the distributor of His graces, the artisan of His
wonders, the co-redemptrix of the human race, the mediatrix
of men, the exterminator of the enemies of God, the faithful
companion of His grandeurs and triumphs.

God the Father wants children by Mary until the end of
time. He tells her, "Dwell in Jacob," which means, "Dwell
in My children, My chosen ones, those represented by Jacob;
not in the worldlings, the children of the devil, represented
by Esau."

In the natural order, a child is born of a father and a
mother. It is the same in the supernatural and spiritual gen-
eration. There is a Father—God. And there is a mother—
Mary.

All the true children, the chosen ones of heaven, have
God for their Father, and Mary for their mother. Whoever
does not have Mary for his mother does not have God for his
Father. This is why the wicked, and the heretics and others
who hate or despise or are indifferent toward Our Lady, do

not have God for their Father. If they had Mary for their mother they would love and honor her, as good and true children naturally love and honor the mothers who gave them life.

There is a sure way to find out whether a man is a heretic, the preacher of a false doctrine, an enemy of God, or a chosen soul. The heretic and the enemy of God will show his scorn of the Blessed Virgin, or his indifference to her; or he will try, by word and deed, openly or secretly, to belittle devotion to her. Sometimes he will mask his hatred with arguments that seem very good.

God the Father did not tell Mary to dwell in these, because, alas!, they are Esaus.

God the Son wants to be formed, and to take flesh—so to say—in the members of His Mystical Body, every day, by His dear Mother. He says to her, "Take Israel for your inheritance." That is the same as saying, "God, My Father, has given Me all nations for My inheritance, and all men, the good and the bad. Some I will lead with a rod of gold; the others with a rod of iron. To some I will be a Father and an Advocate. The others I will justly punish. I will be the Judge of all. But you, dear Mother, will inherit and possess only the chosen ones, represented by Israel. As their mother, you will give them birth; you will feed them; you will bring them up. And as their sovereign, you will lead, govern, and protect them.

"This man and that man is born in her," the Holy Ghost sings in the 86th Psalm of David. According to some of the early Fathers of the Church, the first man born in Mary is the God-Man Jesus; the second is a mere man, the adopted child of God and Mary. Since Christ, the Head of mankind, was born in her, the chosen ones who are members of this Head, must necessarily be born in her, too.

A mother does not give birth to the head without the members, nor to the members without the head; otherwise she would, in the natural order, bring forth a monster. In the same way, in the order of grace, the Head and the members are born of the same mother. If a member of the Mystical Body of Christ—a chosen one—were born of any other mother except Mary, who gave birth to the Head, he would be neither a chosen one nor a member of Jesus Christ. He would, in the order of grace, be a monster.

Moreover, Christ is the fruit of Mary still—as heaven and earth continually avow. "And blessed is the fruit of thy womb, Jesus." It is therefore a fact that Christ is as truly the fruit and the work of Mary, for each particular man who possesses Him, as He is for the world in general. Consequently if any of the faithful has Christ formed in him, he may say boldly: "Many thanks to Mary! What I have is hers; and without her it should not be mine." St. Paul's words, "I am in labor until Christ be formed in you," may be applied much more truly to her. ("I give birth every day to the children of God, until Jesus Christ, my Son, be formed in them in the fullness of His age.")

St. Augustine surpasses himself—and me—when he says that all the chosen ones are hidden in the womb of the Blessed Virgin, during this life, to be made into the image of the Son of God. There the good mother keeps them, nourishes them, cherishes them, and makes them grow until she bears them into glory after death—which is really their birthday, as the Church calls the death of the just.

O mystery of grace little known to the chosen ones, and totally unknown to the reprobates!

The Holy Ghost wants to form His elect in Mary and through her. "Send the roots of all your virtues deep into My chosen ones, My beloved, My spouse," He says to her, in effect, "so that they may grow from virtue to virtue and from grace to grace. I was well pleased with you when you practiced the most sublime virtues on earth. Therefore I desire to keep you still on earth—though you remain in heaven. Reproduce yourself in My elect. Let Me be well pleased in them. Let Me see in them the roots of your unshakable faith, of your deep humility, of your constant self-denial, of your sublime spirit of prayer, of your burning charity, of your firm hope, of all your virtues. You are still My spouse, as faithful, as pure, and as fruitful as ever. Let your faith give Me faithful ones, your purity virgins, your fruitfulness My temples and My elect."

When Mary has planted her roots in a soul she works the wonders of grace that she alone can produce, because she never had, and never will have, an equal in fruitfulness and purity. With the Holy Ghost, she has produced the greatest thing that ever was and ever will be, a God-Man. And consequently she will produce the greatest things of future times—the great saints who will come toward the end of the world. No other than this unique and wondrous virgin can produce, in union with the Holy Ghost, such unique and wondrous things.

When the Holy Ghost finds His spouse in a soul He flies there. He enters there in His fullness. He fills that soul completely, according as it leaves room to His spouse. One of the main reasons why He does not now work marvels in souls is that He does not find in them a sufficient union with His faithful and inseparable spouse. I say "His inseparable spouse," because He, the Substantial Love of the

Father and the Son, has never taken leave of Mary since He espoused her; the reason is: she has always been faithful and fruitful.

QUEEN OF ALL HEARTS

These are the obvious conclusions to be drawn from what I have just said:

First of all, Mary has received from God a great domination over the souls of the elect. Unless she had the right and dominion over these souls, through a singular grace of the Most High, she could not dwell in them as God the Father commanded; she could not form them, feed them, give them birth into eternal life; she could not have them for her inheritance; she could not form them in Jesus, and Jesus in them; she could not plant the roots of her virtues in their hearts; she could not be the inseparable companion of the Holy Ghost for all those works of grace.

God, Who gave her power over His only begotten Son by nature, also gave her power over all His children by adoption, not only of the body—which would be little—but of the soul as well. Mary is the queen of heaven and earth by grace, as Christ is king by nature and by conquest.

Now, as the kingdom of Jesus Christ consists principally in the heart, or interior, of man—according to the words, "the kingdom of God is within us"—so does the kingdom of Mary. The Blessed Virgin reigns principally in the interior of man, that is to say in his soul. And in souls she and her Son are more glorified than in all visible creatures; so that, with the saints, we may call her the Queen of All Hearts!

CHAPTER III

NECESSARY TO MAN

Secondly, we must conclude that Mary, being necessary to God in a necessity we call "hypothetical," as a consequence of His will, is much more necessary to men, if they would attain the goal of heaven. We must not, therefore, confuse devotion to her with devotion to other saints. Devotion to her is far more necessary than devotion to them. It is not something superfluous. Many pious and learned men have proved, with invincible arguments, that devotion to Mary is necessary to salvation; and that, on the contrary, not to love her is a sign of depravity and doom.

To All Men

That true devotion to Mary assures one of heaven is proven by prophecies and teachings in both the Old and the New Testaments, confirmed by the examples of the saints, and demonstrated by experience and reason. Even the devil and his devotees, compelled by the power of truth, have confessed this in spite of themselves. Of all the texts I might bring to your attention let me quote only the words of St. John Damascene: "To be devout to thee, O Blessed Virgin, is a weapon of salvation God gives to those He wants to save."

In the chronicles of St. Francis of Assisi it is related that in an ecstasy he was shown a ladder that reached into heaven. Our Blessed Mother was on the top of this ladder. And St. Francis was told that one had to go through her to enter into eternal bliss.

15

And in the chronicles of St. Dominic it is related that once, near the city of Carcassonne, while preaching the Rosary, he came upon a heretic possessed of fifteen thousand devils. These wicked spirits, at the command of the Blessed Virgin, confessed many great and consoling truths about the Rosary and about devotion to the Queen of Heaven. And though they were thrown into confusion and fury by the Virgin's demands, they so praised devotion to her that anyone who loves her at all must shed tears of joy.

Since, then, devotion to Mary is essential to eternal salvation, it is ever more necessary to those called to a particular or special perfection; and I cannot see how one could acquire intimate union with Our Lord and perfect fidelity to the Holy Ghost without acquiring a very great union with Mary and a very great dependence on her.

It is Mary alone who found grace before God without the help of any other mere creature. It is through Mary alone that all those who found grace before God—after her —have found it. It is through Mary alone that future souls will find that grace. She was full of grace when the Archangel Gabriel hailed her. She was abundantly filled with grace when the Holy Ghost overshadowed her. And from day to day, from moment to moment, she has increased this double-fullness of grace.

Thus she has reached a height of grace beyond all human thought or notion. She is not only the treasurer of God's treasures, she is the only dispenser of them. She can ennoble, exalt, and enrich whom she wills. She can lead them into the narrow way to heaven. She can conduct them through the narrow door of life, in spite of all obstacles. And she can give them the throne, the scepter, and the kingly crown!

Jesus is, everywhere and always, the Son and the Fruit of Mary. Mary is, everywhere and always, the tree that bears the Fruit of Life, the true Mother that produces It.

To Mary alone God gave the keys of the cellars of divine love. To Mary alone He gave the power to enter into the most sublime and the most secret ways of perfection. To Mary alone He gave the power to lead others along those paths. It is Mary alone who welcomes the miserable children of the faithless Eve into the earthly paradise where they may walk in all pleasure with God; where they may safely hide from their enemies; where they may delight in the fruits of the Tree of Life, and of "the tree of the knowledge of good and evil"; where they may drink all they wish of the bountiful and beautiful fountains; and where they will have no more fear of death.

She, herself, is this earthly paradise, this blessed and virgin land, out of which the sinners, Adam and Eve, have been driven. She invites there only those she wants, that she may make saints of them.

Throughout the ages, and especially toward the end of the world, the greatest saints will be those most zealous in praying to Mary, and in having her always present as a model to imitate and as a powerful ruler to protect them.

I say this will happen especially toward the end of the world—and this soon—because then the Most High with His holy Mother will form great saints for Himself, saints who will tower in holiness over other saints even as the cedars of Lebanon tower over little bushes. This has been revealed to a holy soul.

These great saints will be chosen to fight against the enemies of God pressing on from all sides. They will be singularly devoted to the Blessed Virgin. They will be illumined by her light. They will be fed by her milk. They will be led by her spirit. They will be supported by her arm. They will be constantly under her protection, so that they will fight with one hand and build with the other.

With one hand they will overthrow and crush heresies, schisms, idolatries, and impieties. With the other they will erect the temple of the true Solomon, the mystical city of God—meaning the Virgin Mother, who is called both the temple of Solomon and the city of God.

By word and example, these tremendous ones will draw the world toward true devotion to Mary. This will bring them many enemies, but it will bring many victories, too. And much glory for God!

This is what was revealed to St. Vincent Ferrer, the great apostle of his age. This is what the Holy Ghost seems to have foretold in the 58th Psalm: "And they shall know that God will rule Jacob and all the ends of the earth; they shall return at evening and shall suffer hunger like dogs and shall go round about the city." The city around which men will circle at the end of the world, to be converted and to satisfy their hunger for justice, is Mary, "the city of God."

Toward the End of the World

The salvation of the world was begun by Mary. It will be brought to fulfillment by her. In the first coming of Christ she kept herself mostly in the shadows, so that men—who then knew little about her Son—might not wander from Him, and from Truth, by attaching themselves too closely and too strongly to her. There was danger of this, because of the beauty with which the Most High had endowed her. One of the early writers, speaking of Our Blessed Lady, declared she might have been accepted "as a goddess!"

Mary must be made better and better known, however, in the second coming of Christ—so that Christ may be better known, loved, and served. There is no longer any reason to keep Our Lady in the background. The Holy Ghost will see to it that His masterpiece is discovered, and known to all the world, in these latter days. He wishes to reveal her in the fullness of her glory because, through her humility, she held herself lower than the dust; and because He wishes to be glorified and praised on her account by all humanity then living.

Mary is the dawn which precedes and discloses the Sun of Justice, Christ, Our Lord. She must be seen by all, so that Christ will be seen.

She is the way by which Christ came to us the first time. She is the way by which He will come the second time. But the manner of His coming will be different than it was on that first Christmas day in Bethlehem.

Mary is the safe path, the direct road, the immaculate highway we must travel to find Jesus. It is through her that souls shining with sanctity must find Him. He who finds Mary, finds Life—the Life, the Truth, the Way. But one cannot find Mary unless he seek her; and he cannot seek her unless he knows her, for nobody searches for an unknown thing. Therefore Mary has to be better known than ever— that the Holy Trinity may be better known, and more universally adored.

Mary must shine more brightly than ever in mercy, in power, and in grace—mercy, that she may save sinners; power, that she may disperse and crush the enemies of God, who will rise in terrible wrath against her children; and grace, that she may inspire and strengthen those fighting in her cause.

She must be as terrible as an army in battle array to the devil and his hosts, especially in these last years of the world. For then Satan, knowing he has little time left, will redouble his efforts to win souls for hell. He will increase his cruel persecutions. And to the true children of Mary, whom he finds harder to overcome than all others, he will offer the most cunning and the most terrible temptations.

One must recall and understand the awful words God spoke to the serpent in Eden. They should be explained for the glory of the Virgin Mary, for the salvation of her children, and for the shame and confusion of the devil. "I will put enmities between thee and the woman, between thy seed and her seed; she will crush thy head, and thou wilt put snares to her heel."

God has declared only one war; but it is an eternal war; and He fights it relentlessly and without any kind of forgiveness. It will increase in bitterness as the earth approaches its end. It is the war between Mary and the devil; between the children and servants of Mary and the children and servants of Lucifer.

God has made His Mother the devil's fiercest foe. From the moment He cursed the serpent in Eden, He put into Mary—though she did not then exist in the flesh—a growing hatred of His fiendish enemy. He gave her also so much knowledge of the devil and his malice, and so many fearful weapons to use against him, that the lord of hell fears her more than all men and angels; and, in a way, more than God Himself!

The anger, the hatred, and the power of God are, of course, infinitely greater than those of Mary. But Satan finds her more fearsome. Being such a proud spirit, he suffers awful shame at being defeated and punished by such a humble little servant of God. Her humility hurts and abases him much more than the divine power. And then, too, God has given Mary such dominance over the fallen angel that when she sighs for a soul it affects the devil more than all the prayers of all the saints; and one single threat from her inflicts more agony on him than all the torments of hell. The demons themselves have been compelled again and again to admit this through the speech of souls "possessed."

What Lucifer lost through pride, Mary won through humility. What Eve lost through disobedience, Mary saved through obedience. By heeding the serpent, Eve caused the downfall of herself and all her children. She delivered them into the serpent's power. Mary, having completely surrendered herself to God, saved her children and servants, with herself, and consecrated them to God.

True, God has declared only one war; but He has put enmities between Mary and the devil, and between her seed and the devil's seed; and He has sown secret hatreds and dislikes between the followers of Mary and the followers of the devil. They do not, frankly, love each other—these two armies. They do not have any natural attraction or friendliness toward each other.

The children of Satan, the friends of the world—it's the same clan—have always persecuted those who belong to the Queen of Heaven, as Cain persecuted his brother Abel, and Esau his brother Jacob. They will be more cruel in their persecution as time goes on. Cain and Esau represent the children of the bottomless pit. Abel and Jacob stand for the chosen, the elect. Mary, the humble one, will always conquer the angel of pride; and she will crush his head, where his pride dwells.

She will always show her children the snake in the grass, waiting with malice for the unwary. She will render the devil's mines harmless. She will foil his plots. And, until the end of time, she will protect her own from the talon and the claw.

Her might will be seen especially in those years to come, when Satan will lay his snares against her heel.

By her heel is meant her humble slaves, the poor children she will use in her army against the infernal foe. They will be little in the eyes of the world, poor, and humble—like the heel, which is small and humble, and is trodden upon by the body.

However, these little ones who comprise Our Lady's heel will be rich in the grace of God, which Mary will give them. They will be most holy. They will be superior to all other creatures by reason of their zeal. And they will be so strongly armed that, in union with Mary, they will crush the devil's head — with the humility of the heel — and proclaim the triumph of Jesus Christ.

To sum up, God wants His Mother to be better known, and to be more loved and honored than she has ever been. And this will be accomplished, if the chosen ones, with the grace and light of the Holy Ghost, take up the practice I will disclose to them in the following pages.

Then they will see this lovely Star of the Sea as clearly as their faith permits; and she will guide them into a safe harbor despite all perils. They will know the grandeurs of their sovereign lady. They will consecrate themselves entirely to her, as her subjects, her slaves of love. They will know the delight of her favors, her tenderness, her motherly care.

And they will love her as simply as children love their mother.

They will realize how much they need her help. They will know the abundance of her mercies. They will go to her in all things as to their dear advocate. They will realize she is the shortest, safest, straightest, easiest route to Jesus; the perfect route. They will deliver themselves to Mary, body and soul, without any reserve, that they may belong in the same manner to her Son.

Who will these followers of Mary be, these children, servants, and slaves? And what will they be?

They will be brands of fire, ministers of the Lord who scatter the fire of divine love everywhere. They will be like arrows in the hands of the mighty Mother of God, sharp arrows that will transfix her enemies. They will be the children of Levi, well purified by the fire of great tribulations and clinging closely to God. They will carry the gold of love in their hearts, the frankincense of prayer in their minds, and the myrrh of self-denial in their bodies. They will bring to the poor and the humble everywhere the fragrance of Jesus. And they will bring to the great, the rich, the proud, and the worldlings, the putrid stench of death.

They will be clouds flying, with great thunder, through the air, moved by the breath of the Holy Ghost. They will be attached to nothing earthly. They will be troubled by nothing material. They will be worried by nothing at all. They will shower down the rain of the Word of God and of eternal life. They will thunder against sin. They will lash the world with storms. They will strike the devil and his legions with their lightning.

They will be the true apostles of that age. The Lord will

speak through them. He will work wonders through them. He will give them strength to despoil His enemies.

They will live without gold or silver—and without worry —in the midst of the other ministers of God. They will be given the silver wings of the dove to help them carry out the works of salvation for the glory of God. They will leave in their trail the pure gold of charity. They will walk in the footsteps of Christ's charity, poverty, humility, and contempt of the world. They will show the narrow path to God. They will not be guided by worldy standards, fears, or cares. They will fear no human being, no matter how mighty or fearful he may be.

The two-edged sword of the word of God will be carried in their mouths as in a scabbard. Their shoulders will bear the blood-stained standard of the Cross. In their right hands they will hold the Crucifix, and in their left the Rosary. The holy names of Jesus and Mary will be written in their hearts. And the modesty and the self-denial of Jesus Christ will be with them always.

These are the great ones that are to come. Mary will give them birth, at the command of the Almighty, that they may extend His empire over that of the impious, the idolatrous, and the Mohammedans; that they may win His enemies to His dominion.

But when or how all this will come about, God alone knows. All we can do about it is be silent, pray, sigh, and wait. It is written:

"Expecting, I have expected."

CHAPTER IV

CHRIST OUR LAST END

WE have discussed the necessity of devotion to Mary. Now, with the help of God, let us see what it consists of. But, before that, let us expose a few important principles which shall throw light on that great and solid devotion I wish to reveal.

Jesus Christ, our Saviour, true God and true Man, must be the aim and end of all our devotions, otherwise they would be false. Christ to us is the beginning and end of all things; or, as scholars say, using the first and last letters of the Greek alphabet, He is our Alpha and Omega. Our sole work, the Apostle reminds us, is to make every man perfect in Jesus Christ; because in Him is all the fullness of divinity, all graces, all virtues, all perfections.

Christ alone is our Master, our Lord, our Head, our Model, our Physician, our Shepherd. He is the Way we must follow, the Truth we must believe, the Life that gives us life. He is our All in all things. He alone is enough.

No other name under heaven has been given for our salvation than the name of Jesus. God has given us no other foundation for our redemption, our perfection, our glory. Any edifice not built on this strong Stone is built on quicksands and cannot endure. Any Christian who is not united to Him, as a branch to the vine, will wither and fall away—fit for nothing but burning.

If we are in Jesus Christ, and He in us, we need not fear damnation. No creature in heaven or earth or hell can harm us, and none can separate us from the love of God, which is in Jesus Christ. Through Christ, in Christ, and with Christ, we can do all things. We can render homage to the Father in unity with the Holy Ghost, we can make ourselves perfect, we can be a good influence on our neighbor leading him to eternal life.

If, then, we wish to establish a strong true devotion to Mary, it is only that we may the better establish a perfect devotion to her Son. We wish only, through Mary, to find a sure and easy way of finding Jesus. If devotion to Mary could in any way lessen devotion to her Son we should have to reject it. But the contrary is true, as I have shown, and as I will show more clearly. Devotion to Mary is vital if we should discover, know, love, and faithfully serve Jesus Christ.

O most lovable Jesus I turn for a moment, here, in prayer to You!

Let me complain to Your divine Majesty that so many Christians, and even some of the most scholarly among them, do not know of the bond that exists between You and Your holy Mother! You are, O Lord, forever with her; and she is forever with You. She cannot exist without You. She is so completely transformed in You through grace that she no longer is herself alone. You, my Jesus, alone live and reign in her, more perfectly than in all the angels and saints.

Ah, if man only knew what glory and love You receive in Mary they would have far different sentiments about You and her. She is more closely united to You than light to the sun, than heat to fire. She is more intimate with You than all the angels and the saints. She loves You more ardently and glorifies You more perfectly than all the other creatures put together.

Yes, I complain, my adorable Master. I complain indeed. Is it not a pitiful thing—and is it not also amazing—to see the ignorance of all men here below, the darkness that shuts Your holy Mother's glory from them? I do not mean idolators and pagans who do not know You, and therefore never heard of Mary. I do not even refer to those heretics and schismatics who have left You and Your holy Church, and, therefore, do not care particularly for either of You. I speak of Catholics —and even of some of the doctors of the Catholic Church. It is of them I complain!

They profess themselves Your followers, Your disciples, Your teachers. But they know neither You nor Your Mother, except in a manner of speaking—a dry, prosy, sterile, uninspired manner of speaking. They pretend to teach others the truths of the Church—though these truths do not set them afire, do not even appeal to them! They speak but rarely of Mary, and about the devotion one must have for her. They fear, they say, that people may abuse this devotion, may offend You by practicing it!

These men cry out against the little ones who love Your Mother and who preach devotion to her. They would hush up these loving ones. They mouth a thousand reasons in protest against too much talk of the Blessed Virgin Mary—the handmaid of the Lord, the most marvelous work of the Creator, the beloved spouse of the Holy Ghost, and Thine own immaculate Mother! They counsel destruction of all devotions to Mary—whereas they should encourage all the nations to love and honor her.

These men pretend to be Your champions, Lord—Your champions against Your own dear Mother! They say devotion to her lessens devotion to You. But it is plain to see they do not love You either. If they loved You at all, they could not help but love Your Mother. They are, arrogantly, even against devotion to the Rosary and the scapular!

These, they say—these unimaginative, pompous, proud people—are devotions fit only for weak and womanish minds, for the ignorant and superstitious. One can be saved without all "this silliness," they maintain. Should they encounter one who loves the Rosary they seek to change him. "Forget the beads," they say. "Recite the seven penitential psalms." If they encounter one who loves Our Lady, they frown, and bid him pray to Jesus Christ alone.

Sweet Lord, dear Son of Mary, do these people please You? Can anyone please You who does not dearly love Your Mother? Does devotion to her really prevent devotion to You? Does Mary take away from You, ever, the honor due You? Does she have a clique of her own? Is she a total stranger to You? Does it anger You that one should love her? Does anyone, by giving himself to her, and by loving her, separate himself from You?

Guard me, Lord! Guard me from the sentiments and prejudices of these so-called scholars who work so hard at turning people away from the devotion to Your God-loved Mother. Guard me; and give me some share in the feelings of gratitude and love You have for Your Mother, so that I may love and glorify You all the more, in proportion as I imitate You in Your love and gratitude to her!

And now, Lord Jesus, as if I had said nothing at all in honor of Your holy Mother, give me the grace to praise her worthily! In spite of all her enemies—who are, of course, Your enemies—let me shout from the rooftops: "Let no one presume to hope for the mercy of God who slights or offends God's Mother!"

Let me love You ardently, Jesus, that I may obtain, from

Your mercy, a true devotion to Your most holy Mother. And let me set the whole world afire with this devotion, that all on earth may love You ardently, too. For this end I offer you the prayer of St. Augustine:

"Thou art Christ, my holy Father, my tender God, my great King, my good Shepherd, my only Master, my best Helper, my most beautiful Beloved, my living Bread, my Priest forever, my Guide homewards, my true Light, my holy Sweetness, my straight Way, my shining Wisdom, my pure Simplicity, my peaceful Harmony, my complete Protector, my good Portion, my eternal Salvation. . . .

"O Christ Jesus, lovable Lord, why have I loved, why have I desired, in my entire life, anything but Thee? Jesus, my God, where was I when I was not with Thee? Henceforth, O all my desires, become red hot! Flow forth unto the Lord Jesus! Run! Ye have lingered long enough. Hasten where you are going! Seek Whom you are seeking! O Jesus, anyone who does not love Thee—let him be anathema! Anyone who does not love Thee, may he be filled with bitterness!

"O sweet Jesus, may every good feeling, suitable to Your praise, love Thee, delight in Thee, admire Thee.

"God of my heart, my portion, Jesus Christ, may my heart faint in its spirit, and may You live in me. May the live coal of Thy love burn in my soul, and may it grow into a raging fire. May it burn constantly on the altar of my heart. May its fervor glow in my inmost being. May it blaze in the hidden depth of my soul. And, in the day of my consummation, may I be found consumed with Thee. . . . Amen."

I give this admirable prayer here so that you may say it every day to ask for the love of Jesus—which we must seek through His most sacred Mother.

SLAVES OF JESUS AND MARY

From the part played by Christ in our redemption we must conclude that we do not belong to ourselves, but wholly to Him; as St. Paul says, as His members and His slaves whom He bought at a great price, the price of His blood.

Before we were baptized we belonged to the devil as slaves. Baptism made us slaves of Christ. We must, therefore, live, work and die for the sole purpose of giving Him some profit from us. We must glorify Him in our bodies. We must make Him reign in our souls because we are His conquest, His acquired people, His inheritance.

The Holy Ghost compares us to trees planted along the waters of grace in the field of the Church; trees that must yield fruit in season; and to the branches of a vine, of which Christ is the stock, and which must bear good grapes; and to a flock, of which Christ is the Shepherd, which must multiply and provide food; and to a rich farm, where Christ is the Plowman, in which the seed increases itself and produces bounteous crops. Christ cursed the barren fig tree and condemned the useless servant who hid or wasted his talents. This indicates that He expects some fruit from us, some good works. Good works belong exclusively to Him. We have been created "in good works in Jesus Christ," by which words the Holy Ghost tells us not only that Christ is the sole Principle and must be the last End of all our good works, but also that we must serve Him not only as hired hands, but as slaves of love.

Let me explain. There are two ways of serving, here on earth; of belonging to someone and depending on his authority. One is to be a paid servant. The other is to be a slave. In Christian countries a person promises to serve another for a time, for wages or profits or rewards of some other kind. But through slavery one binds himself to a master—or is bound—for life. He is wholly dependent. He may not claim any wages nor seek any reward. He is as much a piece of property as a horse or a cow.

There are three kinds of slavery; the slavery of nature, the slavery of force, and the slavery of the will—or voluntary slavery. In the first sense all creatures are slaves of God, for "the earth is the Lord's, and its fullness." The devils and the damned are slaves in the second sense. The just and the saints are God's slaves in the third sense.

Voluntary slavery is the most perfect kind of slavery, and the most glorious to God. He looks at the heart. He asks for the heart. His name is "God of the heart," that is, of the loving will. Through this slavery one chooses God and the service of God above all things, even though nature did not oblige us to do so.

A servant does not give his employer all he is, and all he has, and all he may acquire; but the slave gives himself in complete surrender with all he is and owns and hopes to be and have. A servant demands wages; a slave can demand nothing, no matter how hard he works, nor how diligently, nor how profitably to his owner. A servant may leave one employer for another; a slave has no rights of this or any other sort. The employer of a servant has no right to wound or kill him; but the master of a slave may lawfully sell or slay him.[1] A servant works only for a time; a slave forever.

There is nothing on earth that gives one more completely into the power of another than slavery. There is nothing, among Christians, that binds us more absolutely to Christ and Mary than voluntary slavery. Christ gave us an example of

---

[1] *De Montfort, of course, refers here to pagan law.*

this, since He took the form of a slave, for love of us. And Mary also gave us an example of this when she called herself the handmaid, the servant and slave, of the Lord. St. Paul proudly calls himself the slave of Christ. And several times in the Sacred Scriptures the Christians are referred to as slaves of Christ.

The Latin word, *"servus,"* did not mean "servant" in the sense of that word today; for there were no servants then, there were only slaves, or freedmen who served. The Catechism of the holy Council of Trent, in order that there might be no doubt as to our being slaves of Christ, used the word *"mancipia"* and not *"servi"* or *"servus."* There is only one meaning to *mancipia*—"slaves."

So I say we must belong to Jesus Christ and serve Him not only as hired servants but as loving slaves, as slaves prompted by a great love to surrender ourselves, asking the sole honor of belonging to Him. Since Baptism changed our status from slaves of the devil to slaves of Christ, we must remain slaves of Christ or again become slaves of the devil.

What I say, in the absolute sense, of Jesus, I say, in a relative sense, of Mary. Jesus, having chosen her as the inseparable companion of His life, His death, His glory and of His power in heaven and on earth, gave her—by grace—in relation to His majesty, all the rights and privileges He possesses by nature.

As the saints put it, all that belongs by nature to God belongs by grace to Mary. Therefore, they add, since both have one and the same power, and one and the same will, they have the same subjects, the same servants, and the same slaves. One may then make himself the slave of Mary to become more perfectly the slave of Jesus.

Our Lady is the means Christ used to come to us. She is

not like other creatures who might draw us away from God, should we become attached to them. She will bring us closer to Him. Her strongest desire is to unite us to her Son. And her Son's strongest desire is that we come to him through her. This is the way to please and honor Him—as it would please and honor a great king if one became the slave of His queen. That is why the holy Fathers, and St. Bonaventure after them, assert that the way to draw closer to Christ is to come closer to Mary.

And, since the holy Virgin is the sovereign queen of heaven and of earth, it must be true—as St. Anselm holds, and Saints Bernard, Bernardine and Bonaventure—that she has many subjects and slaves as there are creatures. "Behold, all things, including Mary herself, are subjected to the power of God. And behold, all things, God included, are subject to the Virgin's power!" Is is not reasonable then, that among so many slaves of constraint, there would be some slaves of love, some who choose to be slaves of Mary?

What? Shall men and devils have their willing slaves, and Mary none? Shall an ordinary king see to it that, for his honor's sake, his queen has slaves, with full power of life or death over them—and Our Lord, the best of all kings and the best of all sons, resent the fact that His Mother own slaves? Does Christ respect and love His Mother less than Assuerus loved and honored Esther, or David Bathsheba? Who would dare to say, or even think, such a thing?

But where does all this lead me? Why do I strive to prove so obvious a thing? If some men protest our calling ourselves slaves of Mary, what does it matter? Let us call ourselves slaves of Jesus, which is the same thing, since Jesus is the fruit and the glory of Mary. And this is what we do perfectly through the devotion we will discuss later.

CHAPTER V

MARY OUR MEDIATRIX

WE need Mary in order to die to ourselves.

Our best deeds are ordinarily soiled and corrupted by the evil that taints our humanness. When one pours clear pure water into a dirty and foul-smelling container, or wine into a cask spoiled by the vintage it held before, the good water and the good wine suffer contamination.

When God pours His grace into the vessel of the human soul—the heavenly dew, the pure living water, or the delicious wine of His love—His gifts are sometimes corrupted by the bad odor that original and actual sins have left within it; or by the bad leaven and the evil dispositions which are the lees or sediment of sin. Our actions, even those born of the most sublime virtues, are affected by the dregs of sin.

Therefore, in order to acquire perfection, which is attained only by union with Jesus Christ, it is of the greatest importance that we empty ourselves of all the bad in us. Otherwise, God, infinitely pure and infinitely intolerant of even the least stain in our souls, will not unite Himself to us, will shut us out of His sight.

In order to empty ourselves of ourselves we must first realize fully, through the light of the Holy Ghost, exactly what we are. We are prone to wickedness. We are unable to do anything good for our salvation. We are weak in all things. We are inconstant at all times. We are unworthy of any grace.

The sin of our first parents has spoiled us all, soured us,

corrupted us, and puffed us up as bad leaven sours, puffs up, and corrupts the dough. The actual sins we have committed, venial or grave, though they have been forgiven, have increased our lusts, our weaknesses, our inconstancy, our natural wickedness. And they have left their slime within our souls!

Our bodies are so corrupt that the Holy Ghost calls them bodies of sin, conceived in sin, nourished in sin, capable of breeding any sin—bodies subject to a thousand ills which engender nothing but sores, scabs, vermin, and rottenness!

Our souls, united to our bodies, have become so carnal that the soul is spoken of as flesh. "All flesh, having corrupted its way. . . ."

We have, for our own, nothing but pride and blindness in the mind, weakness and inconstancy in the heart, lust and passion and diseases in the body. We are by nature more proud than peacocks, more attached to the earth than toads, more ugly than goats, more envious than snakes, more gluttonous than pigs, more quick than tigers to red anger, more lazy than turtles, more weak than any reed, more inconstant than any weathercock. We have within ourselves only nothingness and sin; and we deserve only the wrath of God, and everlasting hell!

Considering this, is it any wonder that Our Lord bade His would-be followers to renounce themselves and hate their lives—that he who loved his life would lose it, and that he who hated his life would save it?

The Infinite Wisdom, Who does not give commands without a reason, bids us to hate ourselves only because we deserve to be hated. Nothing is so worthy of love as God. Nothing so merits hatred as ourselves.

Now, in order to become empty of self, we must die to

ourselves daily. We must disown the operations of the powers of our souls and the senses of our bodies. We must see as if we saw not, hear as if we did not hear, use the things of this world as if we did not use them. If the grain of wheat falling into the earth does not die it will not bear fruit. If we do not die to ourselves, and if our holiest devotions do not lead us to this necessary and fruitful death, we will bear no worthwhile fruits and our devotions will be worthless.

All our works of holiness can be soiled by self-love and self-will. In this case the greatest sacrifices we may make and the best actions we may perform will be abominations in the sight of God! And, dying, we will find ourselves without virtues, and without merits. We shall have not one spark of that pure love known to those who have died to themselves and have buried themselves with Jesus Christ in God.

We must choose, among all the devotions to Mary, the one that will most certainly lead us to this death to self. That devotion will be the best for us, the most sanctifying. We must remember that not all is gold that glitters; not all is honey that is sweet; not all is essential to our being holy that is easy to do, or that is done by the most people.

As in nature there are secrets to learn in a short time, with little trouble, and at little cost, and things that we find easy to perform; so, in the order of grace, there are secrets that can be learned without any trouble, and things that can be easily accomplished—such as emptying ourselves of self, filling ourselves with God, and becoming perfect. The practice I intend to disclose is one of these secrets of grace. It is unknown to most Christians. It is known to a few devout souls. It is loved, and practiced, by a very, very few!

But before I tell you about it, here is another truth you must understand:

It is this: it is more perfect (because it requires more humility) to approach God through a mediator and not by ourselves. If we rely upon our own efforts to reach God—we being so corrupt—it is certain that even our noblest attempts will fail to induce Him to unite Himself to us and to answer our prayers.

It is not without reason that God gave us mediators. He knew our unworthiness and incapacity, and was moved to pity. In order to give us access to His mercies, He provided us with powerful advocates. To neglect these, and to go to God without a recommendation from any one of them, is to go without humility and without respect to God most high, most holy! It is to make the King of Kings of less account than an ordinary prince of the world, whom we would not dare approach without asking someone to request an audience for us.

Jesus is our Advocate, our Mediator of redemption with God the Father. It is through Him we must pray; we and all the rest of the Church Militant, and the Church Triumphant. It is through Him that we are given access to the Father's majesty. And never must we appear before the Father without leaning on the merits of the Son, and indeed without being clothed with those merits, as little Jacob was clothed with the skins of young goats when he came to receive his father's blessing.

But do we not need a mediator with the Mediator Himself?

Is our purity so great that we could be united to Christ directly, and by ourselves? Is Christ not God, equal to the

Father in all things? Is He not the Holy of Holies and as worthy of respect as His Father?

Should we have less respect and less fear for the majesty and holiness of Jesus than for that of His Father— Jesus Who made Himself our Bail, our Bondsman, and our Mediator with His Father, because of His infinite love for us, and because He wanted to appease His Father's anger and redeem us from our debts?

Let us say loudly with St. Bernard that we need a mediator with the Mediator; and that the one most able to fulfill this office is Mary. Through her the Mediator came to us, through her we must go to the Mediator.

If we are afraid of going directly to Jesus Christ, God, either because of His infinite grandeur, or because of the vileness of our sins, let us implore the help and intercession of our mother, and His Mother, Mary. She is good. She is tender. There is in her nothing austere, nothing forbidding, nothing too sublime, nothing too bright. Seeing her, we see our pure nature. She is not the sun that might dazzle us by its rays. She is more like the moon, which receives and tempers the light of the sun and adjusts it to our dim perception.

Mary is so loving she sends no one away who asks her intercession, even though they be the worst of sinners. As all the saints declare, never has it been known that any one who had recourse to her with trust and perseverance was left unaided. She is so powerful with God that He has never denied one of her requests. She has but to present herself with a prayer before her Son. At once He grants it. He is always vanquished by the womb that bore Him, the breasts that nourished Him, and the lips and eyes that worship Him as they pray.

All this is taken from St. Bernardine and St. Bonaventure. According to them we have three steps to ascend to reach God. The first, which is the closest and most suited to our littleness, is Mary. The second is her Son. And the last is, of course, God the Father. In order to go to the Father we must first go to the Son, our Mediator, our Redeemer. In order to go to the Son we must first go to Mary, our mediatrix, our intercessor. Through the devotion I shall tell you about, this order is perfectly maintained.

Considering our frailty, it is difficult to preserve the graces we have received from God.

The treasures of God, worth more than heaven and earth, are kept in such fragile vessels—in corruptible bodies and fickle souls which a breath disturbs and depresses! The devils, subtle thieves, watch us constantly, hoping for the right moment—when we are not expecting attack—to strip us of all these. They circle about us. They swoop to devour us. Through one sin, we may lose, in a moment, all the graces and merits we have piled up through many years.

The malice of the devil, his tricks, and the number of evil spirits under his command, should make us fearful of suffering this appalling loss. People richer in grace than we, higher in sanctity, and more experienced in the spiritual life, have been caught thus, unawares, and robbed. Ah, how many tall cedars of Lebanon have crashed; how many blazing stars have fallen from the sky, their brilliance fled! What is the reason for such calamities? Not lack of grace but lack of humility.

These people considered themselves stronger and more self-sufficient than they were. They thought they were relying only on the grace of God! They thought their houses strong enough to protect heaven's gifts. They thought their coffers stout enough to resist all tampering. They thought themselves bold enough to stand guard over all they possessed.

And the most just Lord left them to themselves, and permitted them to be despoiled.

Alas, had they known the true devotion to Mary, they would have entrusted all their riches to her. And the powerful and faithful Virgin would have kept these riches as her very own and held them against all foes.

It is difficult to persevere in sanctity. That is because of the strange corruption of the world. The world is so filthy it seems to sully all of us. Even the hearts of religious are smeared with dust, if not with mud or slime.

It is something of a miracle if one stays firm in the torrent without being carried away; if one sails through a stormy pirate-ridden sea without being shipwrecked, drowned, or attacked by corsairs; or if one walks safely through a countryside reeking with pestilence. And it is the Virgin Mary who works the miracle. She works it for those children who serve her the right way.

This being clear, we must now, certainly, choose that right way, the true devotion, to her.

CHAPTER VI

FALSE DEVOTION

FALSE devotions, which might easily fool me, are more numerous today than ever before. The devil, that sly forger and counterfeiter, has doomed many souls with his subtle frauds; and he will doom others. He amuses his dupes and lulls them into sin by making them think that a few prayers, even badly said, and a few exterior devotions—inspired by himself—are the best "devotions."

The ordinary counterfeiter seldom troubles to imitate base coins. It is not profitable. He wants something that can pass for gold or silver. The devil seldom bothers about spurious devotions. He does concentrate all the power of evil on counterfeiting the gold and silver coins of devotion to Jesus and Mary.

It is important, therefore, that we should know these bogus Marian devotions lest we be swindled by them. And it is more important that we should learn which, of all the true devotions to Mary, is the most perfect—the most pleasing to Our Lady, the most glorious for God, and the most sanctifying for ourselves so that we may adopt it.

There are, I find, seven kinds of false devotees and false devotions to Mary. I class the devotees as critical, scrupulous, exterior, presumptuous, inconstant, hypocritical, and interested.

The critical are usually proud scholars, people of independent and self-satisfied minds. Deep down in their hearts they may have some devotion to the holy Virgin; but they object to most of the humble and simple ways of showing love that humble and simple people use.

41

They discredit all miracles, and all stories of the Virgin's power, even those taken from the chronicles of religious orders and told by trustworthy authors. They are shocked at seeing someone kneeling before a picture or a statue of Mary. They say this person is worshiping an idol.

They say that, so far as they are concerned, they do not care for public demonstrations. And when one mentions to them something said about Mary by the Fathers of the Church, they sneer. The saint was exaggerating, they say. Or he was "merely orating." And sometimes they twist the saying of the saints into sinister meanings.

These false devotees, these proud and critical and worldly ones, are greatly to be feared. They do tremendous harm to devotion to Our Lady; and frequently in pretending to destroy its "abuses," they succeed in affecting the piety of others.

Scrupulous false devotees are those who imagine they are dishonoring Mary's Son by honoring Mary. They fear they may belittle the One by exalting the other. They cannot stand that men should praise the Mother of God as the great saints have praised her. They rant and rave when they see more people kneeling before the Virgin's altar than before the Blessed Sacrament—as if one were opposed to the other, and as if those who pray to Mary do not pray to Jesus through her.

These people do not want their friends to talk so much about the Queen of Heaven, nor to address her so often. "Why so many Rosaries?", they ask. "Why so many Marian confraternities and exterior devotions? This is ignorance. It is making a mummery of religion. Let's have the real thing. Let's have devotion to Jesus Christ." They name the Lord without taking off their hats, or bending their heads. "Let's

preach Jesus, nothing else. That is a solid devotion. Jesus
is our only Mediator."

What they say about Jesus is true; but in the way they
apply it to prevent devotion to the Mother of Jesus—using it
as a pretense of fostering a greater good—one finds a cunning
snare set by the devil. We never give more honor to Jesus
than when we give honor to Mary. We honor her only to
honor Him. We go to her only to find Him. Holy Church,
with the Holy Ghost, blesses Our Lady first and Jesus second.

"Blessed art thou among women, and blessed is the fruit
of thy womb, Jesus."

Not that Our Lady is more than Christ, nor even equal to
Him. To say that would be the rankest heresy. But it is true
that in order to bless Jesus more we must first bless Mary.
Let us say, then, with all her true devotees, to confound the
scrupulous and false:

"Blessed art thou among women, and blessed is the fruit
of thy womb, Jesus."

Exterior false devotees are those for whom Marian devotion consists only in outward show. They relish this sort of
thing because they have no interior spirit. They will say many
Rosaries—hastily. They will hear several Masses in a morning, without attention. They will march in processions, without fervor. They will enroll themselves in all Mary's confraternities, without reforming their lives, stifling their passions, or imitating Mary's virtues.

They like the form, the spectacle, the display, without at
all relishing the substance. If they do not "feel" during their
religious practices, they think they are not "doing" anything.
They get upset. They drop everything. Or they say their
prayers by fits and starts.

The world is full of this sort of people. And nobody is

more quick to assail men of real prayer, who, while not at all disregarding the exterior practices, do pay attention to the essence of the devotion.

Presumptuous false devotees are sinners abandoned to their vices. Or they are worldlings who pass as Christians and children of Mary. With the semblance of devotion to her they conceal pride, avarice, impurity, drunkenness, anger, profanity, gossip, and all sorts of injustices. They sleep peacefully with their evil habits. They do not give themselves the trouble of amending their lives.

What's the use? they ask. Aren't they devoted to Mary? They think they are. So God will forgive them. They think He will. They will not die without the Sacraments. They think they won't. They will not be damned. They think they won't. Don't they say the Rosary, when they think of it? Don't they fast, sometimes, on Saturdays? Don't they belong to a Marian confraternity ? Don't they wear a scapular—or even a slave bracelet to show they belong to Mary? (Some even say her Little Office once in a while!)

When one tells them their devotion is nothing but an illusion of the devil, and a presumption that may damn them to hell, they do not believe. God is merciful and good, they answer, and He didn't make us in order to damn us. There is no man without sin, they argue, and as even a sinner can make a good act of contrition on his deathbed, that is enough.

Some, confirming themselves in their folly and blinding themselves completely to their peril, defend their loose conduct with stories, true or false—it matters little which, it seems—about the Blessed Virgin's "marvelous" rescue of sinners, even those who had died in mortal sin.

Some sinners, these presumptuous ones have read, or heard, were raised from the dead long enough to enable them to confess their sins and receive absolution. Our Lady, according to these tales, did this because the poor sinners had, at some period of their lives, said prayers to her daily, or practiced certain devotions to her. Therefore, the presumptuous expect, she will do the same for them!

Nothing in Christianity is more abominable than this presumption. It is satanic. For who can truthfully say he loves Mary when he mercilessly taunts, scourges, and crucifies her Son by his continued sins? Who would dare to say that?

I say that to so abuse devotion to Mary—which is the holiest and most fundamental of all, after devotion to Our Lord in the Blessed Sacrament — is to commit a horrible sacrilege.

The worst and least pardonable sacrilege is to make a bad Communion. The one committed by the presumptuous is the next worst.

I admit that it is not absolutely necessary to avoid all sins in order to be truly devoted to Mary; although it is desirable. But one must, at least—mark my words carefully—one must at least shun all mortal sins and do violence to himself that he may not sin. Also he must enroll in some confraternity of Mary, recite the Rosary daily, and perform other Marian devotions. All this is a wondrous help in the conversion of sinners, even the most hardened.

Should you be such a sinner, should you have one foot already dangling in the abyss, I advise you to do all these things; but only with the intention of obtaining, through Our Lady, the grace of contrition for your sins, the grace to make a good confession, and the grace to overcome your evil habits.

Inconstant false devotees are those who are devout to Our Lady at intervals, and according to their own whims. At times they are fervent. At times they are tepid. Now they are ready to do anything in the service of the woman best beloved in heaven and on earth. Now they are bored with praying to her.

They will, at first, embrace all devotions to her, join all her societies and sodalities. Then they neglect their rules, their prayers. They change like the moon. So Mary puts them under her feet with the lunar crescent. They are fickle and not worthy to be counted among her faithful and constant slaves and servants.

It is better not to take upon oneself so many prayers, so many devout practices. One does much better with a few devotions, if he performs them with fidelity and love.

Hypocritical false devotees seek to hide their ugliness of soul from the eyes of others by flying the banner of the Virgin most pure.

And interested false devotees are more devoted to themselves than to the Lady whose name they invoke. They want something from her. They want to win a lawsuit. They want to escape some danger or some just punishment. They want to be cured from some disease. They have a lot of needs—without which, they would forget all about her.

These, and all the other shams, are acceptable neither to God nor to His holy Mother.

Let us take care not to be numbered among those who criticize everything and believe nothing, those afraid of too much devotion to Mary, those interested only in the shadow and not in the substance, those who presume on Our Lady's tender care and Our Lord's mercy while they rot in their sins, those as shifty as weather vanes in their likes and dislikes, those who dress themselves in Mary's livery or flaunt her glorious blue banner only to fool others into thinking they are good—the hypocrites!—and those who never go to the Queen except to ask for something or to demand it of her.

CHAPTER VII

TRUE DEVOTION

HAVING disclosed and condemned false devotees and false devotions, it is time to say something about true devotion—which is interior, tender, holy, constant, and disinterested.

True devotion is interior because it springs from the heart and mind. It wells up out of the esteem one has for the Virgin Mother, the high ideas he has formed concerning her splendors, and the love he bears her.

It is tender, and as trustful as a child is toward his mother. It prompts one to seek her in all his needs of body and spirit, and to ask her help in all things, everywhere and always. It beseeches her to banish his doubts, correct his errors, and keep him on the right path. It implores her protection against temptations. It begs for her strength in moments of weakness. It cries to her to lift her child up when he has fallen. It impels one to rush to her for encouragement when despair confronts him; and to be freed from scruples and consoled in pain and woe. It inspires one to hasten to her in all spiritual weathers, and that without the least fear of annoying her or displeasing her Son, God.

It is holy because it induces us to imitate Mary's virtues and to avoid sin. It speeds one toward acquiring something of her profound humility, her lively faith, her blind obedience, her continual self-denial, her constant prayer, her divine purity, her flaming charity, her heroic patience, her angelic sweetness, and her supernatural wisdom—the ten principal virtues of Our Lady.

It is constant, for it urges one to maintain his devotion

and never abandon it. It strengthens one in goodness; it furnishes him with enough courage to fight the fashions and opinions of the world, the flesh in its passions and agonies, and the devil and his temptations.

A true lover of Mary is not a changeling. He is not glum, not scrupulous, nor afraid. Oh, he sometimes falls. He sometimes is less ardent than at other times. But if he falls, he gets up again and stretches out his hand to his mother. And if he loses the taste and the "feeling" he has known, he is not at all affected thereby; for he lives on his faith in Jesus and Mary and not on the feelings of his body.

True devotion is disinterested, for it impels us to seek God alone, in His Mother, and not to seek ourselves. A true lover does not serve his beloved in a spirit of profit or gain, either for body or soul. He serves Mary because she is most worthy of being served; and because she is, at once, the Mother, the daughter, and the holy spouse of God. God alone is the reason. God in Mary. The true lover does not love her because she is good to him or because he expects some good from her. He loves her because she is so superbly lovable. He serves her faithfully, in dryness and boredom as in sweetness and fervor. He loves her as much at Calvary as at Cana.

How pleasing, how precious, to Mary and to God, is such a soul! And how rare!

It is in the hope that such souls—souls that seek not their own pleasure in serving Mary and Jesus—will be numerous in time to come that I am writing down here what I have taught and preached in public and private so many years.

I have already said many things about Our Lady. I have many more to say. And there is much I must omit—through ignorance or inability, or lack of time—in this attempt to fashion true lovers of Mary and true disciples of Jesus Christ.

But my labor will be well rewarded if this little book falls into the hands of one nobly born! By that I mean one born of God and Mary, not of blood; not of the will of the flesh nor of the will of man.

Provided that it reveals to him, through the grace and inspiration of the Holy Ghost, the value of the true and solid devotion I am about to describe, I shall be indeed rewarded!

If I were sure that my guilty blood could help men understand in their hearts the truths I am now writing about my dear mother and sovereign queen — of whose servants and slaves I am the least and lowest—I would use it to write these words.

My sole hope is to reach some souls, who, by their faithfulness to this devotion, will repay her for the losses she has suffered through my ingratitude and infidelity.

I feel now more than ever inclined to believe all the signs that are so deeply etched into my heart—and which I have for so long sought from God—all the signs that indicate Our Lady will have many more children, servants, and slaves of love than she has ever had; and that, through them, Jesus Christ, my dear Master, will reign more than ever in human hearts.

And yet I foresee that frenzied beasts will come, in fury, to tear these pages into shreds with their diabolical teeth— and me also, whom the Holy Ghost has used for the writing of them. I foresee they will bury this book—if they do not rend it—in the darkness and silence of some old vault or strong box, so that it may not be read. I foresee, furthermore, that they will attack and persecute those who read it and put it into practice.

No matter. So much the better. I am encouraged. This foresight encourages me and makes me hope for a great success, namely, that it will recruit great armies of brave soldiers, men and women in love with Jesus and Mary, to fight against the world, the flesh, and the devil, in the perilous days to come.

Whoever reads, let him understand! Whoever accepts, let him accept!

There are several interior practices of true devotion to Mary. Here, briefly, are the main ones:

1—Honoring her as the worthy Mother of God, esteeming her above all others as the masterpiece of grace and the first after Jesus Christ, Who is true God and true Man.

2—Meditating on her virtues, her privileges, her actions.

3—Contemplating her splendors.

4—Offering her acts of love, praise, and thanks.

5—Invoking her aid with one's whole heart.

6—Offering oneself to her, and uniting oneself to her.

7—Doing everything with the object of pleasing her.

8—To begin, to continue, and to finish each action through her, in her, with her, and for her that we may do them through Jesus, in Jesus, and with Jesus, and for Jesus, our Last End. (We shall explain this last practice.)

True devotion has several exterior practices, too.

1—Enrolling oneself into Mary's confraternities and joining her congregations.

2—Entering the religious orders instituted in her honor.

3—Proclaiming her praises.

4—Fasting, giving alms, denying oneself in her honor.

5—Wearing her liveries, such as the scapular and the Rosary, or the little chaplet, or a chain in token of slavery to her.

6—Reciting, with attention, devotion, and modesty, either five decades of the Rosary daily, or the entire fifteen decades.

One might also say a chaplet of six or seven decades in honor of the number of years Mary is believed to have spent in this valley of tears; or the "little crown" composed of three Our Fathers and twelve Hail Marys, in honor of the crown of twelve stars that encircle the Virgin's head, or the twelve great privileges she enjoys. Likewise one may say the Little Office, or the "Little Psalter" St. Bonaventure composed for her—which is so moving that one cannot recite it without feelings of tenderness. One may, in addition, say fourteen Our Fathers and Hail Marys in memory of Our Lady's joys and sorrows; or other prayers of devotion.

7—Singing spiritual canticles to her, or having them sung to her.

8—Genuflecting or bowing to her every morning, while greeting her with the hymn "Hail Mary, Faithful Virgin," with the idea of obtaining, through her, faithfulness to the graces God may give us throughout the day; and saying good-night to her with the hymn "Hail, Holy Queen Mother of Mercy," and asking God to forgive, through her, the sins committed during the day.

9—Taking care of her confraternities, adorning her altars when possible, and seeing that her pictures and statues are well displayed and clean.

10—Carrying little images of her, as powerful weapons against evil spirits

11—Painting pictures of her, or having them painted, and making them public; also making her better known everywhere.

12—Consecrating oneself to her in a special and solemn manner.

There are many other practices of true devotion to Mary which will make us saints, if they be performed with the pure intention of pleasing God, of uniting us to Christ, and of edifying our neighbor; and if the performance is completed with attention, with devotion, with no willful distraction, in a modest and respectful bodily posture, and without haste.

Now, having read almost all the books on devotion to Mary, and having talked with the holiest and most learned people of our day, I say with all sincerity that I have never known any devotion like the one I now wish to reveal to you. None other requires more sacrifices for God. None other makes a soul more empty of self and self-love, or keeps it more faithfully in the grace of God. (And the grace of God in that soul unites it more perfectly and more easily to Jesus. It gives more glory to God, greater sanctity to the soul, and more benefits to our neighbor.)

Since the essence of this devotion lies in the interior which it ought to form it will not be easily understood by all. Some will stop at its outer doors and will go no further. They will be in the majority. A few will enter within. But some will mount only the first step.

Who will climb to the second? Who will reach the third? And who will advance so far as to make this devotion his permanent way of life?

None but those to whom the spirit of Jesus reveals this secret will penetrate the depths of this devotion and remain there. He Himself will guide these truly faithful souls, to make them grow in virtue, in grace, and in light, until they come to the transformation of themselves in Him, and to the fullness of His age on earth and of His glory in heaven.

PART II

CHAPTER VIII

PERFECT CONSECRATION TO JESUS CHRIST

As all our perfection consists in being conformed, united, and consecrated to Jesus, the most perfect devotion is, naturally, that which conforms, unites, and consecrates us most perfectly to Him.

And, as Mary is, among all creatures, the one most conformed to Jesus, it follows that devotion to her is the one that best consecrates and conforms a soul to her Son. Therefore, the more a soul is consecrated to Mary, the more it is consecrated to Jesus.

This is why perfect consecration to Jesus is nothing less than perfect consecration to Mary—which is the devotion I preach and teach—or, let us say, the perfect renewal of the vows and promises of Baptism.

This devotion consists in giving oneself entirely to Our Lady, so that we may belong entirely to Jesus through her. We must give her our body, with all its senses and members; our soul, with all its faculties; our goods or riches and all we shall acquire; and all our inner assets, such as merits, virtues, and the good works we have done or may do. We must give all we have, in the order of nature and the order of grace; and all that may come to us even in the order of glory. We must reserve nothing, be it a penny, a hair, or the least good deed. And we must do this for eternity, without expecting or claiming any other reward than the honor of belonging to Jesus through and in Mary.

We must here remark that there are different values in good works. One is a satisfying, or atoning, or liberating value. It is used to remit, or annul, or forgive, in part or in whole, the punishment due to sin. Then there is the prayer value by which we may obtain some new measures of grace. Finally, the meritorious value merits grace for us now and eternal glory later.

Now, in this consecration of ourselves to Mary, we give her all our merits, graces, and virtues. These she cannot transmit to others; for, properly speaking, they cannot be communicated. Only Jesus, Who made Himself our surety with His Father, has the power to communicate His merits.

Our Lady can and does keep these merits, graces, and virtues safe for us in the strong box of heaven. Furthermore she increases them and gives them the pure lustre they lacked. (I will come back to this later.)

But she can and does use the satisfying, atoning values as well as the prayer value of our good works, applying them where she will, for the greater glory of God.

What are the consequences of this consecration?

First, we give to Jesus all we can give Him; and in the best way we can give it, since we give it through His Mother. We give much more than we do by all other devotions. That is because in these other devotions we give but part of our time, part of our good works, part of our merits and atonements. In true devotion we give all, even to the right of disposing of our interior riches, and of the treasures of expiation earned day by day in our good works. This is not done even in religious orders.

In the religious life one gives to God his earthly goods by the vow of poverty, his body by the vow of chastity, and his will by the vow of obedience. Sometimes he gives his physical freedom by the vow of enclosure. But he does not give God the right to dispose of the value of his good works. He does not strip himself of what is most dear and precious to the Christian, his merits and his acts of atonement or reparation.

Secondly, a man who has thus voluntarily sacrificed and consecrated himself to Jesus through Mary cannot any longer dispose of the value of any of his good works. All his sufferings, borne joyfully or with resignation, all his thoughts, and all the good he does, belong to Mary. And she may dispose of everything according to the will of her Son, for His greater glory.

This dependence, however, does not interfere with the obligations of our state in life—for instance in the case of a priest who is obliged, at times, to apply the satisfactory and prayer value of the Mass to some particular person—for the consecration is made according to the order of God and the duties of one's state.

In the third place, we consecrate ourselves to Mary and Jesus at one and the same time—to Mary as the perfect means by which Jesus unites Himself to us, and us to Himself; and to Jesus as to our Last End, our Redeemer, and our God, to Whom we owe all we are.

I have said this devotion could be called a perfect renewal of the vows and promises made by us, or for us, in holy Baptism. Since every Christian was a slave of the devil before he received the sacrament, he has, in Baptism, either through his own lips or the voices of his godparents, solemnly renounced Satan and all his works and pomps. He has taken Jesus for his Master and Sovereign Lord. He has become a slave of love, utterly dependent on that Master.

This is what we do through this devotion.

We renounce the devil, the world, and self; and we give ourselves entirely to Jesus through Mary. We do even more; because in Baptism, usually, we give ourselves by proxy, whereas now we do it in our own persons. We do it voluntarily. We do it with full awareness of what we are doing.

In Baptism one does not give himself to Jesus through Mary, at least not explicitly, nor does he give Him the value of his good works. After Baptism we are perfectly free to apply the value of our good works and prayers to the relief of the souls in purgatory, for instance; or to offer them for those we love; or to keep them for ourselves. Not so in true devotion. Here we do give ourselves along with the value of all our actions to Jesus through His Mother; and we are no longer free to distribute our spiritual coins.

St. Thomas says that at Baptism we take a vow to renounce the devil and his pomps. And St. Augustine says that this vow is the greatest and most necessary . . . "the greatest vow, by which we vow to remain in Christ." Theologians say the same thing . . . "the principal vow is the one that we make at Baptism."

Yet who has kept this vow? Who keeps the promises made in that holy Christening? Do not most Christians prove unfaithful to these promises?

Whence comes this universal disorder if not from our continuous neglect and forgetfulness and disregard of these promises and pledges, and from the fact that scarcely anyone keeps the contract with God which he made through his sponsors?

The Council of Sens, convoked by order of Louis the Debonair in an attempt to remedy the great disorders of Christendom, decided that the main cause for such widespread evils was man's forgetfulness and disregard of his Baptismal vows. And the best remedy it found was a renewal of those vows.

The Catechism of the Council of Trent, faithful interpreter of that holy assembly, exhorts pastors to recommend such a renewal to their flocks, and to remind them that they are bound "forever to our Redeemer and Lord, as His slaves!"

Now, if the Councils, the Fathers of the Church, and experience itself, all show that the best way to remedy the disorders of Christians is to remind them of the obligations they incurred at Baptism, and to ask that they put their promises into operation, is it not reasonable that we should do it in this perfect way—in this consecration to Our Lord through Mary? I say "in a perfect way" because one takes the perfect way to consecrate himself to Jesus; and that way is Mary.

One cannot argue that true devotion is new, or that it is "indifferent." It is not new, since the Councils, the Fathers, and many ancient authors, speak of this consecration to Our Lord, of this renewal of Baptismal vows, as something long practiced, and something all Christians were advised to follow. Nor is it a matter of indifference, since the main source of disorders, and consequently the damnation of Christians, comes from forgetfulness of this practice and indifference to it.

Some may say that since true devotion makes us surrender the value of all our good works, prayers, charities, and penances, it renders us incapable of assisting the souls in purgatory or helping our parents, friends, and benefactors.

Let me answer that.

It is impossible to believe that those near or dear to us should suffer any loss because we have consecrated ourselves thus, without reserve. To credit such a thing would be to insult the power and goodness of Jesus and Mary, Who will

surely manage to help those we love—using either our own
paltry spiritual revenues, or others we know not of.

This practice does not prevent us from praying for others,
the living or the dead, although the actual applying of our
good works depends upon the will of Mary. On the contrary.
It should encourage us to pray with more confidence. Imagine
a rich man giving his entire fortune to a great prince, to
honor him. Could he not confidently ask that prince to help
some friend in need? The prince would even find pleasure
in helping the person named, for it would prove his gratitude
toward the one who beggared himself through love. The
same thing must be said of Jesus and Mary. They will not be
outdone in generosity.

Someone may say, "If I give Mary all the value of my
good actions, and she distributes them here and there, I will
have to suffer a long time in purgatory, because I shall have
no way of shortening my stay."

This objection, which comes from self-love, and from
ignorance of God's liberality and Mary's gracious generosity,
destroys itself. A soul gives everything without reserve, who
breathes nothing but God's glory and the reign of Jesus
through His Mother, and who sacrifices himself completely to
gain that glory and that sovereignty—do you think he will
suffer greater punishment than others in the next world for
having been more disinterested and more generous than others
in this one? Far from it. It is toward souls like this that Our
Lady and Our Lord are most generous, in this world and the
next; in the order of nature, in the order of grace, and in the
order of glory!

CHAPTER IX

PERFECT SERVICE

WE must now consider the motives that commend this devotion to us, the wonderful effects it produces in faithful souls, and the practices it requires.

THE FIRST MOTIVE

One cannot, on earth, conceive any higher employment than the service of God. The least servant of God is richer, more powerful, and much nobler than all the kings and emperors on earth—unless these rulers are also servants of God. Then how rich, how powerful, and how noble is that servant of God who has given the utmost possible, and without condition! Such is the soul who has dedicated himself to the King of Kings through Mary. All the gold on earth and all the beauties of heaven cannot repay him.

Other sodalities, congregations, confraternities, or associations established in honor of Christ and His Mother, and which accomplish so much good, do not require their members to give everything without reserve. They prescribe certain performances, entail certain obligations, but their adherents are otherwise free to do what they wish; and the time outside that devoted to the aims of the societies is theirs to spend as they please.

But in true devotion there is no such limitation. All our words, actions, thoughts, and sufferings are given. At all times and for all time—we do not even have to think about it—whether we watch or sleep, whether we eat or drink, whether we accomplish great or little things, everything we do belongs, in very truth, to Jesus and Mary (unless we have expressly taken back the gift we so freely and generously made). This is no small consolation.

Moreover, as I have already said, true devotion, more than anything else, helps rid us of a certain subtle attachment that creeps into the best of our works. Jesus grants us this immense grace as a reward for the heroic and disinterested act by which we surrendered to Him, through Mary, all the value of our good works. If, even in this world, He gives a hundredfold to those who leave material and perishable goods for love of Him, how many hundredfold will He not give those who sacrifice even their interior spiritual treasures!

Jesus, our divine Friend, gave us Himself without reserve; His Body, His Soul, His graces, and His merits. As St. Bernard puts it . . . "with the whole of Himself He bought the whole of me." Is it not just then, that out of sheer gratitude, we should give Him all we possibly can? He was generous to us. Let us be generous to Him. Then we will find Him even more generous; while we live, when we die, and for all eternity, Jesus gives to those who give!

THE SECOND MOTIVE

Here is the motive that shows us how essentially just it is, and how profitable, for a Christian to consecrate himself wholly to Mary that he may be the more perfectly consecrated to Christ.

Our Master deemed it good to enclose Himself in the womb of Mary, as a captive, as a living slave; and to be subjected and obedient to her for thirty years of His life. Our human mind staggers when we seriously consider this. Incarnate Wisdom did not will to give Himself directly to men, although He might have done so. He willed to give Himself to men through Mary. He did not will to be born a perfect man, independent of all others. He willed to be an infant, dependent for everything on His Mother's care.

Infinite Wisdom, burning with desire to glorify His Father and save the human race, found no better or quicker way of doing so than by submitting Himself completely to His Mother, not only for the first few years of His life—as other children do—but for thirty years!

And He gave His Father more glory during those years of dependence and submission than He would have given by spending that time in preaching, working miracles, and converting all mankind.

Otherwise, He would have done all these things!

What immeasurable glory a soul gives to God when it follows the example of Jesus, and submits itself to Mary!

The example of Jesus is unmistakable. And we know it. So why should anyone think there was a better or easier way to glorify God than by submission to Mary?

Remember what you have read about the Holy Trinity and dependence on Mary. God the Father gave His Son through her; and still does. He begets all His children by her. God the Son was formed through her, to be given to the world. He is still formed and brought forth daily through her, in her union with God the Holy Ghost. It is through her alone that He transmits His virtues and merits. It was only through her that the Holy Ghost formed Christ, through her that He forms the members of the Mystical Body and bestows His gifts and favors.

Here are the many and eloquent examples of the Three Divine Persons in God. Would it not be sheer madness for

us to ignore Mary, or try to do without her? Should we not
indeed consecrate ourselves to her, offer ourselves in sacrifice
to God through her, and depend upon her to bring us to God?

Let me cite a few quotations.

"Mary has two children, a God-Man and a man; the one
she bore physically, the other spiritually" (St. Bonaventure
and Origen).

"This is the will of God: that all goods come to us through
Mary. Whatever hope, grace, or other heavenly gift we receive, let us understand that we owe it to her" (St. Bernard).

"All gifts, virtues, and graces of the Holy Ghost are given
by her hands, to whom she wills, when she wills, as she wills,
and as much as she wills" (St. Bernardine).

"Thou wert unworthy of receiving; therefore Mary hath
been given to thee, that thou mightest receive through her
whatsoever thou wouldst receive" (St. Bernard).

God knows we are unworthy of receiving His graces directly from His hand; so He gives them to Mary, that we may
receive through her all He wants to give us. He also finds
His glory in receiving through her hands the thanks, the respect, and the love we owe Him. It is therefore most just that
we should imitate Him, so that, as St. Bernard puts it, "grace
may come back to its Author through the same channel by
which it came to us."

This is what we do in true devotion. We consecrate all
we are, and all we possess, so that Our Lord may receive,
through Mary, all the gratitude and glory due Him. We deem
ourselves unworthy to come close to His infinite majesty, and
incapable of doing so, by ourselves. That is why we have recourse to His Mother—His and ours, too.

In addition, this is a practice of great humility, a virtue
most dear to God. A soul that exalts itself humbles God. A

soul that humbles itself exalts God. The Almighty resists the proud and gives His grace to the humble. If you humble yourself, if you believe you are unworthy of appearing before Him, of drawing near Him, He will humble Himself to come to you. He will take pleasure in you. And He will, in spite of yourself, exalt you. On the contrary, when you venture toward God boldly, without a mediator, God flees; and you cannot reach Him!

O how precious a humble heart is in His sight! It is to such humility that true devotion leads, since it teaches us never to approach the throne of God save through Our Lady. The Lord is merciful and sweet; but to appear before Him, or to talk to Him, or to give Him anything, or to unite and consecrate ourselves to Him, we need the help of Mary.

THE THIRD MOTIVE

Our Lady, seeing that you have given yourself entirely to her, will give herself—O ecstasy beyond words!—entirely to you.

She will surrender you with her graces, adorn you with her merits, support you with her power, enlighten you with her light. She will inflame you with her love. She will shower all her virtues on you, humility, faith, purity, and all the others. She will make herself your surety with Jesus. She will supply all that is lacking in you. She will be your dear self with her divine Son.

Just as the consecrated one is all Mary's, Mary is all his. And we can say of him what St. John says of himself: "The disciple took her for his own."

This brings into a true soul a great trust in his Lady, a great abandonment toward her, and a great distrust, contempt, and hatred of himself. He no longer relies on his own dispositions, intentions, merits, virtues, or actions—for he no longer has them. He has sacrificed them to Jesus through Mary. All he has left, his sole treasure, is Mary.

Now he can go to the Lord without servile fear and without scruples. Now he can pray to God with great confidence. Now he, too, can address to Mary the beautiful words spoken by the devout Abbé Rupert—alluding to Jacob's victory over the angel with whom he wrestled. "O Mary, my Princess, immaculate Mother of the God-Man, I desire to wrestle with that Man, the Word of God, your Son—but strengthened with your merits, not my own."

What power before Jesus has that man who is covered with the merits and the love of Mary, the worthy Mother of God! (St. Augustine tells us she has lovingly vanquished the Almighty!)

When one has given God all his good works through Mary, she purifies them, makes them beautiful, makes them acceptable to God. She washes all the stains of self-love from them, and all the blemishes that creep, unnoticed, into even the noblest of our human actions. As soon as her pure hands touch the offerings of her children they cleanse them, make them perfect.

She makes them much more beautiful by adorning them with her own perfections!

It is as if a farmer, wishing to gain the favor of his king, went to the queen and offered her an apple—which was all he had in the way of revenue—that she might present it to the monarch. The queen, having graciously accepted the pathetic offering would serve it to the king on a beautiful golden dish.

Thus the apple, though not exactly the thing to give a

king, would become a present worthy to be given him. In itself it was only an apple. On the golden dish, and in the hands of the beautiful queen, it became fit even for royalty.

Mary does not keep for herself any of the gifts presented to her. She gives everything to her Son. What one gives her, she gives, necessarily, to Jesus. If one praises and glorifies her, she praises and glorifies God. When Elizabeth praised her, Mary sang her Magnificat. "My soul doth magnify the Lord. . . ."

No matter how small or poor the gifts offered to the King of Kings, the Holy of Holies, Mary makes each and all acceptable to Him. When one, relying only on himself, makes the Lord a present, He may reject it, as in ancient days He rejected the sacrifices of the chosen people because there was self-will in their offerings. But when one presents something through the virginal hands of His Mother, he takes God by His weak side, so to say.

The Lord does not so much consider the gifts as He does the woman who places it before Him. He does not consider whence the offering comes so much as He considers the person by whom it comes.

As she is never treated discourteously by her Son, never reproved, never refused, Mary is able to make everything she presents, big or little, acceptable to Him. If she gives it, He is glad to take it. St. Bernard, leading souls to perfection, used to say, "When you want to offer anything to God, be sure to offer it through the most agreeable and most worthy hands of Mary—unless you wish it to be rejected."

The little ones of this world, when dealing with the great, make use of any mediator they can find. Why should we not do likewise, in the order of grace, when dealing with God? He is infinitely above us. We are like specks of dust before

His face. But we have an advocate so dear to Him she does not know of a refusal, so wise and holy she knows all the secrets that win His heart, and so kind and loving she never rejects anyone. She welcomes all, no matter how wretched or how small.

THE FOURTH MOTIVE

If we are faithful to true devotion we may be assured that the value of all our good works are being used for the greater glory of God. Who, nowadays, ever works for this end—though we all are obliged to do so? Why don't we? It is either because we do not know where the greater glory of God is to be found, or because we do not look for it. But Our Lady knows. She does nothing except for that greater glory. So, a perfect servant of hers, one fully dedicated to her, may be assured that all his thoughts, words, and deeds, are being used for this purpose—unless, alas, he positively revokes his offering. Can anything be more heartening for one who loves God with a pure and unselfish love, and who prizes the glory of God and the interests of God far above his own?

CHAPTER X

PERFECT WAY

The Fifth Motive

True devotion to Mary is an easy, short, perfect, and safe road to perfection, which means union with Christ. To a Christian, perfection is nothing else than such a union.

It is an easy road. It was opened by Jesus when He came to us. There are no obstacles there to prevent our using it to go to Him.

One may, it is true, arrive at union with God by other roads. But he will encounter many more crosses; he will find deadly perils; and he will have many difficulties to overcome. There will be dark nights, strange fights, bitter agonies. There will be steep mountains to climb, sharp patches of briars and brambles to traverse, and frightful deserts to cross.

The road of Mary is gentle, and more peaceful. One finds there, it is true, great difficulties and fierce battles. But our mother is ever near, to light the darkness, to clear away doubts, to give strength, to banish fear, to help in every way.

The Virgin road to Jesus, in comparison with all others, is a stretch of roses and "bee-trees" packed with wild honey. There have been a few, not many, saints who have walked this way — Ephrem, John Damascene, Bernard, Bernardine, Bonaventure, Francis de Sales. The Holy Ghost, Mary's spouse, had revealed it to them. But most of the other saints, though they had devotion to Our Lady, have taken different paths. That is why they faced such dangers and such difficult trials.

How is it then, a faithful servant of Mary may ask, that
those completely devoted to Mary have many sufferings—and
even greater troubles than afflict those less fond of her? Con-
tradiction, persecution, slander, and hatred attack them. They
walk in interior darkness. They stroll through seemingly end-
less deserts and without a single drop of heavenly dew. If
true devotion makes the road to Christ easier, why are the
devotees so ill-treated?

The reason is that the most faithful servants, being her
favorites, receive more graces and favors from heaven than do
others. That is, more crosses are bestowed on them. But they
carry these crosses with greater ease than others, with more
merit, and with more glory. Where another would fall, or
stop a thousand times to rest and gather strength, they do not
hesitate, they do not fall.

The bitter pills given them are coated with the sweetness
of their holy mother's love, and with the divine love of the
Holy Ghost. They swallow them as though they were candied
nuts.

It is my belief that anyone who wishes to live truly in
Christ, and carry his cross daily, can never carry a heavy
cross—or bear one joyfully to the end—without a tender devotion to Our Lady.

The road is short. One does not get lost. He walks joyfully in it, and therefore speedily. One makes more progress,
in a brief time of submission to Mary and dependence on her,
than in years of self-will and self-reliance. A man obedient
and docile to God's Mother will sing of glorious victories over
the enemy. This enemy will try to keep him off that road, or
to make him turn back. He will even try his best to make
him fall. But with the help and guidance of Mary the obedient one will not falter. He will advance with the stride of a

giant toward Christ—on that same road by which, with giant strides, and in a little time, Christ came to us.

Why, tell me, did Jesus spend so few years on earth? And why, out of these few years, did he spend so many in submission to His Mother?

Though He was so soon consummated, He lived a long life. It was a life even longer than that of Adam, whose shattered house He had come to repair. Yet Adam lived more than nine hundred years!

Jesus lived a long life because He had lived in submission to His Mother, and in union with her, out of obedience to His divine Father.

Scripture tells us that a man who honors his mother is like one who stores up a treasure — meaning that he who honors Mary, his mother, to the point of subjecting himself to her and obeying her in all things, will soon become very rich. He heaps up treasure daily.

There is another Scripture quotation: "my old age is in the mercy of the womb." According to the spiritual interpretation, it is in the womb of Mary that young people mature in light, in holiness, in experience, and in wisdom. There, in a short time, one achieves the fullness of the age of Jesus Christ!

The road is a perfect one by which to reach Christ and be united to Him. Mary is the most perfect creature, the purest and holiest. And Christ, Who came to us perfectly, chose that road. The Most High, the One Beyond All Understanding, the Untouchable God, He Who Is, came down, perfectly and divinely, to us mean little worms through the humble Mary. And He came without losing anything of His divinity. Therefore it is through Mary that we little ones must, perfectly and divinely, and without fear, ascend to Him.

God, Who cannot be held or limited, let Himself be perfectly surrounded and contained by the little Mary; and without losing anything of His immensity.

So we must let the little Mary perfectly contain and form us—and this without any reserve on our part.

The Untouchable God drew near to us, united Himself closely, perfectly, and even personally, to our humanity, through Mary. And He did so without losing anything of His majesty and awe.

So it is through her we must go near to Him, must perfectly, closely, and fearlessly unite ourselves to Him.

He Who Is willed to come to our nothingness and to cause that nothingness to become He Who Is. This He did perfectly, by giving and submitting Himself entirely to the young maiden, Mary; and without ceasing to be, in time, what He is from all eternity. Likewise it is through the same maiden that we, who are nothing, may become like God, through grace and glory. This, by giving ourselves to her so perfectly and completely as to remain nothing, so far as self is concerned, and to be all in her, without any fear of delusion!

Give me a new road to Christ; one paved, say, with all the merits of the blessed, and adorned with their heroic virtues; one lighted by the beauty of the angels; one peopled with all the saints and angels to guide, help, and protect the travelers—give me such a road and I will still choose that of the Virgin. Amen, amen, I boldly say, I prefer the immaculate road, the one without faults of any kind, without original or actual sin, the one without darkness or even shadows.

And when my Lord Jesus in His glory comes once again to earth, as He surely will, He will choose no other way than that of Mary, by which He came so perfectly the first time.

The difference between His first and His second coming is that the first was hidden and secret whereas the second will be glorious and resplendent. But both will be perfect because both will be through Mary.

Here lies a mystery. Let all tongues be silent here!

True devotion is a safe road to Christ, and to that perfection which is union with Him. The practice I teach is not new. It is very old, but one cannot trace its beginnings with precision. It has been in existence though, for the last seven hundred years. St. Odilo, abbot of Cluny, who lived in the eleventh century, was one of the first to practice it publicly in France. Cardinal Peter Damian tells us that in the year 1016 his brother, Blessed Marian, made himself the slave of Mary. He tied a rope around his neck, scourged himself, and placed a sum of money on the altar as a token of his consecration to Our Lady. This he did in the presence of his spiritual director. He remained so faithful to his consecration that Our Lady visited him on his deathbed and promised to reward him in heaven.

Caesar Bollandus mentions a famous knight, Vautier de Birbak, a close relative of the dukes of Louvain, who made the consecration around the year 1300.

The devotion had been practiced privately by many up to the seventeenth century when it became public. Father Simon de Roias, preacher of King Philip III, made it popular in Spain and Germany. At the request of his king he obtained ample indulgences for its devotees from Pope Gregory XV.

Father de Los Rios, of the Augustinians, a friend of Father de Roias, helped spread the devotion by writing and preaching. He composed a thick book called *Hierarchia Mariana* in which he showed as much piety as learning in explaining the excellence, the solidity, and the antiquity of slavery to Mary.

Sometime during the seventeenth century the Theatine Fathers planted the devotion in Savoy and Sicily. Father Stanislaus Phalacius, a Jesuit, furthered it wonderfully in Poland. Father de los Rios, in his book, mentions the names of princes and princesses and cardinals and bishops who embraced it. Father Cornelius a Lapide, a wise and profoundly holy man, and many other distinguished persons have praised the devotion.

Cardinal de Berulle, whose memory is venerated in France, was one of the most zealous in making the devotion known. He succeeded in spite of all the calumnies he suffered. Men accused him of spreading a new idea, a superstition. They used a thousand stratagems—sponsored by the devil—to prevent his sowing the devotion in France. He was very patient with his enemies. He answered their objections powerfully in a little book, showing the devotion was founded on the example of Jesus, on our obligations to Him, and on the vows we made at Baptism. He made it clear that this consecration to Mary is nothing but a perfect renewal of the vows and promises of Baptism.

In the book of Boudon one may find the names of various popes who, far from condemning, have approved the devotion, of theologians who have examined it, of thousands of people who have made it their own, and of the persecutions it has met and overcome. Indeed we cannot see how it could be condemned without destroying the foundations of Christianity.

It is obvious, then, that this devotion is not new. If it is not commonly practiced, the reason is that it is too excellent to be relished by all.

Another reason why true devotion is a safe way to Christ is that it is Mary's task to lead us safely to Jesus; just as it is the object of Jesus to lead us safely to the eternal Father. Have no fear that Mary may be an obstacle to your union with God. How could she be such, who has found grace before God for the world at large and for each one of us in particular? Could she who was filled and overflowing with grace—and so completely united to God and transformed in Him that in a sense He had to become incarnate in her— could she possibly prevent any soul from being perfectly united to God?

It is quite true that the view of other creatures, however holy they may be, might sometimes retard divine union. But not so with Mary, as I never tire of repeating.

One of the reasons so few souls arrive at the fullness of the age of Jesus is that Mary is not well enough formed in their hearts. Who wants ripe and well-formed fruit must possess the tree that bears it. Who wants the fruit of life, Jesus Christ, must have the tree of life that bears Him—Mary. Who desires the operation of the Holy Ghost within him, must have His eternal spouse, Mary—who, as we have said before, makes Him fruitful!

Rest assured then that the more you look at Mary the more surely you will find her Son, Jesus Christ. He is always with her. This thought of Mary in your prayers, meditations, actions and sufferings does not have to be a clear and distinct one. A general and so to speak sub-conscious thought will suffice.

The heavenly Mary, completely lost in God!

There has never been, and there never will be, any creature who can or will so perfectly help us to attain union with God. Nobody is filled with the thought of God except through her. She will not only give you the graces necessary, but she will also protect you from the illusions and snares of the devil. Where Mary is the devil is not.

One of the unmistakable signs that someone is led by the Holy Ghost, is that he has a devotion to Mary, thinks of her often, and speaks of her frequently. A saint said that. He added that just as breathing is proof that the body is not dead, so frequent thoughts of Mary and loving invocation of her name is proof that a soul is not dead.

Mary alone, says the Church—which is guided by the Holy Ghost—has destroyed all heresies. Therefore, though critics deny it, never will any faithful devotee of hers fall into heresy, at least formally. He may err materially. He may mistake a lie for the truth, and the evil spirit for a good one —though he will not be so easily fooled as others—but he will discover his error, acknowledge it, and correct it. Whoever wishes to put aside the fear of illusion, so common to prayerful souls, let him with all his heart take up this devotion. Let him enter this excellent way, the way opened by Incarnate Wisdom. One cannot make a mistake following this path. It is covered with the fullness of grace, and perfumed with the balm of the Holy Ghost. Who walks thereon does not tire nor retrace his steps. It is a short way. It leads us to Jesus in a short time. It is a perfect way, without mud or dust. And it is a most reliable way. It leads us straight and safely to Christ and to eternal life. It does not take us either to the right or to the left.

Let us enter that road and walk it day and night, to the fullness of the age of Jesus.

CHAPTER XI

PERFECT LIBERTY

THE SIXTH MOTIVE

To the faithful ones, true devotion gives great interior freedom, the freedom of the children of God. We make ourselves the slaves of Jesus. He, to reward us, removes from our souls all servile fear and all scruples. He enlarges our hearts and fills them with confidence in God, teaching us to regard Him as a Father. He also fills our souls with a tender and filial love. Without stopping to prove this truth, I will simply relate a fact in the life of Mother Agnes of Jesus, a Dominican nun who died in the odor of sanctity, in 1634, in the convent of Langeac in Auvergne.

Once when she was suffering great anguish of mind, she heard a voice bidding her make herself a slave of Jesus and His Mother, Mary, if she wanted to be rid of her suffering and to be protected from all enemies. She heeded the voice. She gave herself entirely to Jesus and Mary, though up to that time she had no idea what the devotion was.

She found an iron chain and put it around her waist. (She wore it until she died.) As soon as she had done this all her pains and scruples stopped; and she lived in peace. She taught the devotion to many, among them M. Olier, founder of the Seminary of St. Sulpice, and several other priests and seminarians.

One day Our Lady appeared to her and put a golden chain around her neck, to show how happy she was that Mother Agnes had become her slave. Our Lady was accompanied by

St. Cecilia in this apparition. And St. Cecilia said: "Blessed are the faithful slaves of the Queen of Heaven for they will enjoy true freedom. To serve her is to be free."

THE SEVENTH MOTIVE

Another reason to recommend true devotion to us is the good it will do our neighbors. For, by it, out of our charity and through our mother, Mary, we give them the satisfactory and prayer value of all our good works, not excepting even the least good thought and the least little suffering. We agree that all we have earned and will earn in the way of spiritual riches will be used either for the conversion of sinners or the deliverance of souls in purgatory, as Our Lady wishes.

Isn't this perfect love of neighbor? Doesn't it mark the perfect disciple of Christ, whose measure is that of charity? Isn't this the means to convert sinners and to free the poor souls without endangering ourselves through any feeling of pride and without scarcely doing anything but what we are obliged to do by our state in life? We are bound to do all this anyway; but we do it better through this method.

To acknowledge the excellence of this motive one must consider how wonderful it is to convert one sinner, or to send one tortured soul to heaven out of purgatory. It is an infinite good. It is a far greater good than the creation of heaven and earth because one thus gives to a soul the possession of God!

Should we, in all our life, convert only one sinner or deliver only one poor soul, through true devotion, would that not be enough to make any really charitable person among us eagerly adopt true devotion as his own?

We must remember, I repeat again and again, that our good works, passing through the hands of Mary, take on an increase of purity, and therefore of meritorious value. Consequently they become much more capable of relieving those in purgatory or of bringing sinners back to God. The little we give Our Lady unselfishly and with true charity becomes powerful enough to soften the anger of God and obtain His mercy.

Maybe, when a faithful slave of Mary is about to die, he learns that through true devotion he has converted several sinners, and freed several others from the purging flames! This, though he has performed only the very ordinary duties of his state in life!

What joy for him in the day of his judgment! What glory for him throughout eternity!

THE EIGHTH MOTIVE

The most compelling attraction to true devotion is the knowledge that it is an admirable way to persevere in virtue, to remain loyal to Our Lady and Our Lord.

Why is it that so many sinners lapse back into sin after they have been converted? And why is it that the virtuous do not continue to grow in virtue and in grace—and often lose the little goodness they have? It is because man, corrupt, feeble, and inconstant as he is, trusts in himself alone.

In true devotion we put all our trust in Mary. We rely upon her power. We lean on her mercy and love. We know she will not only keep our spiritual riches intact, but that she will embellish and multiply them, in spite of all the enemies trying to wrest them from us. We talk to her, as a child might; something after this fashion: "Mother, I know I have received a lot of graces from God. I know they came through you. And I know I don't deserve all that, nor any part of it.

But listen! I'm too little, too miserable, too mean, and too afraid to keep all these treasures. You keep them for me! Then I shall have nothing to fear—not even myself."

St. Bernard says, "When she supports you, you do not fall; when she protects you, you do not fear; when she leads you, you do not tire; when she favors you, you come safely into the harbor of salvation."

And St. Bonaventure says, "Our Lady is not only maintained in the fullness of the saints, but she maintains and keeps the saints in their fullness, so that this fullness may not wane. She keeps their virtues, lest they fly away. She keeps their merits lest they die. She keeps their graces lest they disappear. She keeps the devils at a distance from them, lest they inflict some harm. And she keeps her Son from striking them when they sin."

Mary is the faithful Virgin whose fidelity restores what was lost through the infidelity of Eve. She obtains fidelity to God, and perseverance in that fidelity, for those attached to her. She has been compared to a firm anchor which keeps a ship from being wrecked in the troubled sea of the world. How many souls are lost for lack of such an anchor!

Happy and blessed a thousand times all those who are thus anchored! They will not lose their riches through storm or wreck. They will come safe to shore.

Mary has also been compared to the ark of Noah. Blessed are they who trust to the virtues of this ark. They will ride without peril over the flood waters of sin which take so many lives. "Those who come to me to work out their salvation shall not sin," says Mary; for we may apply the words of divine Wisdom to her.

Blessed are the unfaithful children of unfaithful Eve who attach themselves to the faithful Mary, the Virgin who remains forever faithful. She loves those who love her. And never will she neglect or lose what has been entrusted to her by those who love her, and whom she loves.

This good Mother, out of pure charity, always receives whatever we deposit with her—and what she has once received as depositary, she is obliged in justice, by virtue of the contract of trusteeship, to keep safe for us; just as a person with whom I had left a thousand dollars in trust would be under the obligation of keeping them safe for me; so that if, by his negligence, they were lost, he would in justice be responsible to me for them. But the faithful Mary cannot let anything which has been entrusted to her be lost through her negligence. Heaven and earth could pass away sooner than that she could be negligent and faithless to those who trust in her.

Poor children of Mary! You are extremely weak. You are dreadfully inconstant. You are, within you, a mass of corruption. You are drawn from the same corrupted mass as all the other children of Adam and Eve. But do not let this discourage or disconcert you. Dry your tears. Rejoice. Bear in mind the secret I have mentioned, the secret that should be known to all Christians, but is known to very few—even among the devout.

Do not leave your treasures in your own safes. They have been broken open many times and robbed of all they held. And they are too flimsy and too small to hold such treasure as you may amass.

Do not pour clean fresh water into filthy or sour-smelling containers. Do not put delicious new wines into casks that once were filled with evil vintages.

You understand me. But let me speak more plainly. Do not entrust the gold of your love, the silver of your

purity, the waters of heavenly grace, or the wine of your
merits and virtues, to inadequate, common, or home-made
safes—to torn sacks, broken chests, cracked bottles, spoiled
barrels and kegs. You are sure to be robbed by the devils
who try, night and day, to break open your strong boxes. Or
you are certain to spoil all the purest gifts of God because
of the contamination of your self-love and your self-will.

Entrust everything to Mary. She is the dwelling place of
the Holy Ghost, the tabernacle of Glory, the sanctuary beyond compare. Since God imprisoned Himself in this beautiful vessel it has become entirely spiritual, and the spiritual
abode of the most spiritual souls. It has become the place
of glory and honor, and the throne, of the greatest among
the saints.

Mary is the house of gold, the tower of David, the tower
of ivory.

O happy the man who gives all to Mary, who entrusts
himself to her, who loses himself in her! He is all Mary's!

And Mary is all his!

With David we can boldly say: "She is mine." With
John, the beloved, we can say, "I have taken her for my
own." With Christ we can say, "All that is mine is thine,
and all that is thine is mine."

Should anyone imagine I speak with exaggeration, and
out of an excess of emotion, he does not, alas, understand
me. He does not understand me because, either he is a carnal
man with no taste for the spiritual, or he is a worldling who
cannot receive the Holy Ghost, or he is proud and critical
and apt to condemn or despise what pertains to the soul.

But those generated not of flesh and blood and the will
of man, but born of Mary and Jesus, will readily understand
and enjoy what I have to say. And it is to these I speak.

But—resuming the subject from the place where I interrupted it—Mary never lets herself be outdone in love or liberality. For an egg she gives an ox, a holy man says.* Consequently, if a soul gives himself to her without reserve; and if he trusts in her, without presumption, while trying to overcome his passions and practice virtue, she will give herself without reserve to him!

So let the faithful servants of Mary say with St. John Damascene, "I will be saved, O Mother of God, trusting you. I will fear nothing, being protected by you. I will fight and rout my enemies, with your help. For devotion to you is a weapon God gives those He wills to save."

* (Editor's Note: In French the word egg rimes with the word ox.)

CHAPTER XII

A PARABLE

OF all the truths I offer concerning Our Lady and her children and servants and slaves, one of the most remarkable is that inspired by the Holy Ghost in the story of Jacob and how he received the blessing of his father, Isaac.

Esau, the first born of Isaac, sold his birthright to his brother Jacob for a mess of pottage. Rebecca, the mother of the two boys, loved Jacob better than Esau. And she took advantage of the sale of this birthright, later, to maintain Jacob's rights. She used a ruse, holy and filled with mysteries.

Isaac, being very old, knew he was soon to die. He decided to give his blessing to Esau, his elder son; whom he loved more than he loved Jacob. He wanted, however, to enjoy a good meal before he gave Esau this blessing, so he commanded him to go out and hunt some game and to make him a savory dish.

Rebecca acquainted Jacob with what was happening, and bade him bring her two young goats. She prepared these as Isaac liked them. Then she clothed Jacob with some of Esau's finest garments, and covered his neck and his hands with the skin of the kids she had killed. Esau was a hairy man; and Isaac, who was blind, knew him only by his voice, the odor of his garments, and the roughness and hairiness of his hands.

Isaac was conquered by Rebecca's stratagem. He knew the voice was the voice of Jacob, but he believed the hands were the hands of Esau. After he had eaten the dish, he kissed Jacob—convinced, from the smell of his garments, that he was Esau—and gave him his blessing, wishing him "the dew of heaven and the fatness of the earth," and establishing him as master and lord over his brethren. . . . "Let people serve thee, and tribes worship thee . . . cursed be he that curseth thee, and let him that blesseth thee be filled with blessings. . . ."

Shortly after Jacob had gone, Esau walked in with the savory dish Isaac had wanted, and asked for his father's blessing. The holy patriarch was shocked when he discovered the ruse that had been played on him. But far from retracting his words to Jacob he confirmed them; for he saw the finger of God in the affair.

Esau roared in anger, loudly accusing his brother, and asked if his father had but the one blessing to give.

(Here, according to the holy Fathers of the Church, Esau became a symbol of those who seek to serve both God and the world, who want the joys of heaven, and the pleasures of earth as well.)

Isaac, moved by the cries of Esau, at last blessed him, but only with a blessing of the earth. He put Esau under the yoke of his brother. This filled the hairy one with such fury that he could scarcely wait for an opportunity to kill. And Jacob would surely have been killed had not his mother protected him with advice and skill. (He had bought the birthright, the blessing. But in Esau's opinion he had grossly deceived Isaac, and had stolen the blessing.)

Before explaining this beautiful story, we must tell you that, according to the interpreters of Sacred Scripture, Jacob is the symbol of the elect, the chosen souls, and of Christ, and Esau of the profligate or condemned. We have but to examine the actions and conduct of each to be convinced of this.

1—Esau, the elder, was strong and sturdy, skillful with weapons, a man who loved to hunt.

2—He almost never stayed at home. He was generally outdoors. He placed his confidence only in his own strength and skill.

3—He was not much concerned about trying to help or please his mother; and he did little or nothing for her.

4—He was so fond of his own mouth, or of food, that he sold his birthright for a mess of pottage.

5—He, like Cain, was envious of his brother, and persecuted him.

This is the usual conduct of the reprobates.

1—They trust to their own ingenuity or brute strength in temporal affairs. They are strong, clever, and bright, when it comes to the things of this world. They are weak and ignorant when it comes to the things of heaven.

2—They spend little time at home—that is, in their souls, which God gave each man as a dwelling place, and to which they could invite Him. God always stays home. That is, He dwells in Himself, and in His chosen ones. The Esaus do not care for spiritual things, and have no interior devotions. They regard religious people as narrow-minded bigots, fanatics, or fools.

3—The Esaus care little or nothing about Mary, the mother of the chosen souls. They do not formally hate her. They may even praise her sometimes. And now and then they may practice some devotion in her honor. But they do not love her. And they do not like anyone else to love her. They find fault with the manner in which some people try to win her affections. They do not believe such devotion is necessary for salvation. They think that by not hating her, or by not openly despising and opposing those who love her, or by mumbling a few Hail Marys—though without any feeling and without any idea of mending their ways—they will stay in Mary's good graces, and so get to heaven.

4—The Esaus sell their birthright, the joys of heaven, for a mess of pottage—the pleasures earth can provide. They drink, they gorge, they make merry, they dance, they gamble, they laugh; but they are not concerned with making themselves worthy of the blessing of their Father in heaven. They think only of worldly things. They speak only of worldly things. They work only for temporal riches, rewards, and honors. For these things, for fleeting pleasures, for fame that vanishes like smoke, or for a high place—which will not last — they sell their heavenly inheritance, their Baptismal grace, their robe of innocence.

5—The Esaus usually hate and despise the Jacobs, persecute them secretly or openly, mimic and insult them, rob them, ruin them, trample them into the dust and walk over them to reach the things they consider worth having in this life—riches, power, luxury, ease.

Now let us consider Jacob in this order.

1—Jacob, the younger brother, was not so sturdy as Esau. He was peaceful and even-tempered. He loved his mother with all a son's tenderness, and liked to stay at home with her. If he went away from the house it was to run an errand for her, or to do as she had bidden. Never did he leave through selfishness.

2—He loved and honored his mother. He was never so happy as when he was with her. He avoided doing anything that might displease her; and did everything he could to help and comfort her. This increased Rebecca's natural love for him.

3—He was subject to his mother. He obeyed her in all

things, promptly, lovingly, and without complaint. He believed all she told him, and did not argue about it. For instance, when she told him to go and get two kids and bring them to her that she might prepare a savory dish for his father, he did not say that one kid would be enough. Without arguing, he did exactly what she wanted him to do.

4—He trusted his mother, and truly relied on her. He went to her when he needed anything, consulting her when in doubt—as, for instance, when he thought that Isaac would curse him rather than bless him. And he believed and trusted her when she said that, in such an event, she would take the curse upon herself.

5—Finally, he imitated, as much as he could, the virtues he saw in her. It seems to me that one of the reasons he spent so much time with her was to study those virtues and practice them—and to keep himself away from bad companions. By this means he made himself indeed worthy of receiving the blessing of his father.

This is the way the chosen souls are accustomed to act.

1—They love to stay at home. That is, they are spiritually-minded. They apply themselves to mental prayer, following the example of Mary, their mother, whose whole glory, during her life, was within; and who loved mental prayer so much.

It is true they often go out into the world. But they do so out of obedience to the will of God and His Mother, and to fulfill the duties of their state in life.

However great their outward works may seem, they prize their inner accomplishments much more. They esteem the progress they make within themselves, in the company of Our Lady. They work there at the supreme task of perfection, compared to which all other works are but child's play.

They see their brothers and sisters at work, "outside," using great strength, amazing ability, and shrewd skill, to win success and the praise and envy of the world. But through the light of the Holy Ghost they perceive that there is more good, more glory, and more real joy in remaining hidden in their retreat, with Christ as their model, in complete and perfect submission to Mary. They see clearly that this is better than to work miracles by themselves.

"Glory and wealth are in her dwelling." Glory for God, and riches for men are to be found in the house of Mary.

Lord Jesus, how lovable are Your tabernacles!

"The sparrow hath found herself a house and the turtle dove a nest for herself, where she may place her young."

O how happy is the man who lives in the house of Mary, where You lived first!

It is only in this house of Mary, this house of the chosen souls, that one receives his strength from You, Lord Jesus. Only there may he ascend to perfection in this vale of tears.

2—The Jacobs truly honor and tenderly love their mother Mary. They love her not only in words but in deeds. They honor her not only outwardly, but also from the bottom of the heart. They avoid all things that might annoy her; and fervently do everything they can think of that will please her. They bring her not two young goats but their bodies and souls—which is what the kids represented. She will make them die to sin. She will strip them of their skins of self-love. And she will prepare a savory dish of them to offer Christ!

She knows better than any other creature the tastes of the heavenly Father; and she knows better than any other how to prepare things for His greater glory. Through her care and her intercession the bodies and souls brought thus to her will be made into an offering worthy of the Father's blessing.

The reprobates say often that they love Jesus and that they also esteem and love His mother. But they do not love to the extent of offering their bodies and souls in sacrifice.

3—The Jacobs are subject and obedient to Mary as to their mother, after the example of Christ. They follow her counsels exactly. Jacob received the blessing almost by a miracle, by doing as his mother advised. The miracle at the marriage feast in Cana furnishes another example. When the wine failed and Our Lady had spoken to Jesus, she said to the stewards near her, "Do whatever He will tell you." Thus they were honored with her Son's first public miracle, the changing of water into wine. In the same way, until the end of time, only those who show perfect obedience to Mary will receive the blessing of God and be honored with His wonders. The Esaus, on the contrary, will lose the blessing, for lack of their submission.

4—The Jacobs trust in the kindness and power of their mother Mary. Unceasingly they turn to her for help. They consider her their guide, the northern star that will bring them to their proper destination. They open their hearts to her in sorrow. They rely on her tenderness and mercy as naturally as infants at a mother's breasts. They take strength from her maternal sweetness in weariness and pain, and comfort in knowing that, through her intercession, their sins will be forgiven. They even lose themselves—O wonder of wonders! — in that loving and virginal bosom, to be set aflame with pure love, to be cleansed of all stain, and to meet Jesus in His fullness—for this is His glorious throne! O happiness beyond compare!

The Esaus trust not Mary but themselves. Like the

prodigal son in the gospel, they eat the food of swine. Like toads they feed on the earth. Like all worldlings they hunger only for visible and material pleasures. They do not know the sweetness of Mary's bosom. They have not the certainty, the absolute trust, the chosen ones enjoy. In misery, as St. Gregory notes, they love their hunger and will not taste the sweetness prepared within themselves, and within Jesus and Mary.

5—Finally, the Jacobs, the chosen, imitate Mary in every way they can. That is what makes them truly happy. This is the infallible sign that they are among the chosen. "Blessed are those who keep my ways." Blessed are those who practice her virtues, and, with the help of grace, walk in her footsteps during life. While they live they will be happy with the favors Our Lady will grant them. They will be much happier than those who do not follow the maiden-mother so closely. And they will be most happy at the hour of death. She will be there with them. So they are assured of a sweet and tranquil departure into eternity. She will lead them herself into the kingdom of heaven.

None of her faithful ones, not one who has tried to imitate her, has ever been lost!

The Esaus, the forsaken, the proud, are miserable in life, in death, and in eternity; because they do not practice Mary's virtues.

How unhappy, O Mary, and cursed are those who abuse your devotion, and who do not keep the commandments of your Son! "Cursed are they who stray from thy precepts." But, O my mother, let me say it with all my heart, how happy those who shun false devotions to you and keep faithful to your ways, your suggestions, your commands!

CHAPTER XIII

THE PARABLE EXPLAINED

Mary loves those who love her. She loves them because she is really their mother. She loves them because, since they are the chosen ones, God loves them. "Jacob I have loved, but Esau I have hated." And she loves them because they have consecrated themselves entirely to her. They are her portion, her inheritance. "Have Israel for thine inheritance."

She loves them more tenderly than all mothers put together. Should you find in the heart of one woman the motherly love of all the other women in the world, you would find one who really loved her brood. Yet Mary loves her children much more dearly than this imaginary woman could love hers.

She loves them not only in emotions but in deeds; for her love is active and efficient, like that of Rebecca for Jacob. Only more efficient and more active. She is alert for opportunities to make them happy, to make them grow, to enrich them. As she sees clearly in God all the good and evil fortunes that are to come, all the blessings and the curses that are to fall on men, she arranges all things for her children, keeping them from evil and showering them with good. "She takes care of our affairs herself," a saint has said.

She gives her children excellent advice. She inspires them to dedicate their bodies and souls to her. She teaches them to love and obey her divine Son and to follow His example. When she does not speak in person she sends the angels as messengers—and they have no greater pleasure than to obey her.

When they have brought to her and consecrated to her their body and soul, and all that depends on them, without excepting anything, what does that good mother do? Just what Rebecca did of old with the two little goats Jacob brought to her: she kills them, makes them die to the life of the old Adam. She flays and strips them of their natural skin, their natural inclinations, their self-love, their own will and all attachment to creatures. She cleanses them of their spots, their vileness and their sins. She dresses them to the taste of God, and for His greatest glory; and as it is Mary alone who knows perfectly what the divine taste is, and what the greatest glory of the Most High is, it is Mary alone who, without making any mistake, can adapt and dress our body and soul for that taste infinitely exalted, and for that glory infinitely hidden.

Once we have made the perfect offering of ourselves and all we have, once we have stripped ourselves of our old rags of self-pride, self-love, and self-will, she gives us new clothes, so that we may not be shamed when we appear before Our Father in heaven.

She gives us the new, beautiful, perfumed garments of Esau—that is to say, of her Son, Jesus. She has them eternally with her. They are ever at her disposal. For, as I have repeatedly said, she is the treasurer and dispenser of all the merits and virtues of her Son; to bestow them where she will, when she will, and as she will.

As Rebecca covered the neck and hands of Jacob with the skins of the little goats, Mary covers her children with the merits and values of her own works. She cleanses them of all imperfections and impurities; and she keeps the good that grace has worked in them. She enhances it to make it the strength and ornament of their necks and hands—meaning she gives them greater strength to bear the Lord's yoke, which presses against the neck, and more skill for the hands, which work for the glory of God and the salvation of their fellow men.

She gives a new fragrance, a new grace, to these clothes and ornaments from her own wardrobe—the virtues and merits she willed her beloved children before her glorious assumption into heaven. (This was revealed to a holy nun.) Therefore all her children, all her servants, and all her slaves, are clothed with her garments as well as with those of her Son. "All her domestics are clothed in double garments." They will have nothing to fear from the cold of Jesus—a coldness as intense and white as snow—which the lost, standing naked before Him, will be unable to bear.

Mary obtains, for those who love her, the heavenly Father's blessing, to which, as younger children, or adopted sons and daughters, they had no natural right or title. She leads each one in his new clothes, his face shining, close to the Father. The Father hears the voice, and knows it—the voice of a sinner. But He feels the hands covered with the skins put there by Mary. He inhales the aroma of the garments. And He accepts with joy the dish prepared by Mary. Then, being aware of the merits of His Son and of His favorite daughter in the sinner, He gives him the double blessing.

Like Isaac He bestows the blessing of the dew from heaven and the blessing of the fat of the land—the blessing of divine grace, and the blessing of the daily bread, a sufficient amount of the goods of the earth. "He has blessed us with all spiritual blessings in Christ Jesus."

He makes these fortunate ones masters over the forsaken, the lost, the doomed. This is not always apparent in this passing world. "How long shall the wicked glory, mouthing insolent speeches?" And, "I have seen the wicked exalted and uplifted." But the mastery is really theirs; and it will be made evident in the next world. "Then will the just rule over nations."

God not only blesses the chosen, in their persons and their goods, but He blesses all who bless them, and curses all who curse them.

The second office Our Lady performs for her loved ones is to take care of both their spiritual and material needs. She not only clothes them in double garments; she also gives them the most delicious foods from the table of God.

She gives them the Bread of Life.

"Children," says Mary, the seat of wisdom, " 'be filled with my fruits.' That is, of course, Jesus, the Fruit of Life, Whom I bore for you. Come, eat my bread, Which is Jesus, and drink the wine of His love which I have mixed for you."

She is generous to her children. She feeds them on Living Bread and they grow fat. And they drink, and are inebriated, with the wine that fosters virgins. She carries her children at the breast. And when the yoke of Christ is put upon them, they barely feel its weight, they have grown so strong.

The third good thing Our Lady does for her own is to lead and direct them safely home; to conduct them through safe roads, holding them by the hand as they traverse the paths of holiness. She steadies them when they are about to fall, raises them if they have fallen. She admonishes them, out of her great love, when they stray from the right direction. And sometimes she chastises them. How can a child obedient to Mary, his mother, his nurse, and his wise director, go astray in the journey to everlasting life?

Follow Mary, St. Bernard assures us, and you will never get lost. Where she leads, neither devils nor illusions are to be found. No true child of hers will be deceived by the evil one and fall into heresy. Heretics, with their subtleties, stay out of her way.

Like Rebecca, Mary protects her children by her ingenuity and constant care. Esau would certainly have killed Jacob, had it not been for Rebecca's resourcefulness and love. Mary, the mother of the children of God, shelters them in the folds of her blue mantle, even as a hen her chicks. She bends down to whisper to them. She yields to all their weaknesses, in order to save them from the vulture or the hawk. She makes herself an army arrayed in battle formation around them.

What shall we fear?

The Queen of heaven would send down millions of angels to the help of her least worthy slave, were it necessary, lest he succumb to the wickedness and overwhelming malice of his foes.

The greatest gift of Mary to her slaves is her intercession. She is constantly pleading with her Son, Who will judge them, for all her loved ones. And she is constantly bringing them into closer union with Him. Rebecca led Jacob to his father's bed. The old man took the boy in his arms and kissed him. Then, smelling his garments, he exclaimed; "The fragrance of my son is the fragrance of earth when the Lord's blessing is upon it."

This fragrance is that of Mary. She is the rich field, the garden full of grace, in which the Father sowed His only begotten Son.

How Christ, Father of the world to come, will welcome the child who has about him the fragrance of Mary! How quickly He will unite Himself to that child! And how closely!

Once she has laden her children with gifts, and has won for them union with Christ and the blessing of the Father, Mary keeps them in Christ, and Christ in them. And she watches always, lest they lose the grace of God and fall again into the embrace of the devil. To the saints she gives perseverance to the end.

This is the hidden and mysterious meaning of the story of Rebecca and her sons, this beautiful old parable of the chosen and the rejected.

CHAPTER XIV

WONDERFUL EFFECTS

Rest assured, my dear friends and neighbors, if you are faithful to the practices of true devotion, both interior and exterior—I will discuss them later—wonderful things will happen to you.

Through the light of the Holy Ghost—Mary, His spouse, will shine it on you—you will know yourself as you are. You will realize you are corrupted by original sin and incapable of performing any good action except through the grace of God. You will despise yourself. You will regard yourself with horror. You will see yourself as a sort of snail, soiling everything with slime; or as a venomous snake or unwholesome toad. But the humble Virgin will make you share in her humility. So, while you will despise yourself and love to be despised, you will not despise anyone else.

Our Lady will give you a share in her faith, which was greater than that of all the patriarchs, prophets, and saints. In heaven she does not need faith, for she sees all things in God through the light of glory. Yet God permitted that she should keep her faith, that she might give it to the Church Militant. The more Mary loves you, the more surely you will act by faith. Yours will become a faith so pure you will scarcely bother about the extraordinary favors God sometimes gives His beloved, such as ecstasies, for instance. Yours will be a faith animated by charity. You will do everything through no other motive than pure love. It will be a faith firm as a rock, and as unshakable. And it will make you firm and constant in the most terrific storms.

It will be a positive faith, far-seeing. It will be a pass key into all the mysteries of Christ, into the very heart of God.

It will be a brave faith. You will hold it high, a burning torch. It will be your life, your secret treasure of divine wisdom, your all-powerful weapon. By it you will be able to enlighten those sitting in the darkness of the shadow of death, enkindle the luke-warm to renewed ardor, and restore life to those whose souls are dead through sin. By it you will be able, with soft and tender words, to transform hearts of marble and to overthrow the proud tall cedars of Lebanon.

The mother of fair love will rid your heart of all scruples and silly fears. She will so widen it that you may run, with the holy freedom of the children of God, along the ways of her Son's commandments. She will fill it with her treasure, pure love; so you will be governed not so much by the fear of God as by the love of Him. She will make you see God as your Father, and you will try at all times to please Him. You will talk to Him with confidence, with the simplicity of a child. If, unfortunately, you offend Him, you will humbly beg His pardon, stretch up your hand to His, that He may grasp it again, and, without discouragement, continue walking with Him.

Our Lady will put into your heart great confidence in God and in herself. You will no longer be going to Jesus by yourself, but through her. And besides, you will be clad in her great merits; therefore you will be able to say to God, "Behold Your handmaid, Mary; be it done to me according to Your word."

Let me say again that, since you have given yourself so completely to Mary, she will give herself to you. She will give you herself in a mysterious, but real, way, so that you will be able to tell her, "I am yours"; or, with St. John, "I have received you, Mother, as my own."

You may say with St. Bonaventure, "Behold, my Lady, my salvation! I will trust in you and have no fear, because you are my strength and my praise in the Lord."

He says also, "I am yours and all I have is yours, O glorious Virgin, blessed above all. I will place you as a seal upon my heart because your love is strong as death."

And with David you will be able to say; "Lord, my heart is not lifted up, mine eyes not raised from the earth, my mind does not dwell on high things, on marvels that are beyond my reach. Bear me witness that mine were humble thoughts, that my soul was never exalted with pride. The thoughts of a child newly weaned toward its mother, this is all my soul knows of recompense." (Ps. 130)

What will still increase your trust in her is that, since you have unburdened yourself of yourself and given Mary all that is good in you—to dispose of as she may—you will have much less trust in yourself. What a consolation it is for a soul to know that the treasure of God—which contains everything most precious to Him—is his own treasure too!

And the soul of Mary will transmit itself to you to glorify the Lord. Her spirit will take the place of yours, to rejoice in God, her Saviour—provided you keep yourself faithful to the practices of this devotion. "May the soul of Mary be in each one to glorify the Lord; may the spirit of Mary be in each one to rejoice in God."

A saintly man who was all wrapped up in Mary used to say: "When will the happy time come when Mary will be sole queen over the hearts of men and bring them into subjection to her Son? When will the time come when souls will breathe Mary as the body breathes air? Then will wonderful things happen in these lowly places. The Holy Ghost, finding His spouse reproduced, as it were, in every soul, will penetrate them fully and fill them with His gifts . . . to produce wonders of grace."

My dear ones, when will men see this blessed time, this age of Mary, this era when the many souls chosen by her and given her by God, will lose themselves in the abyss of her heart, will become living reproductions of her to love and glorify Jesus Christ?

The time will come only when men learn the devotion I teach; when they learn it and practice it!

Lord, that Thy kingdom may come, let Mary's kingdom come!

If Mary, the tree of life, is well tended in your soul, she will bear her fruit in due time. And this fruit is Jesus.

So many seek Jesus, one way or another. But though they try hard they do not find Him. They have labored much in their quest, but gained, perhaps, only a glimpse of Him.

Walk in Mary's immaculate way. Take the divine practice I teach. And you will find Him. Night or day, you will seek Him in a holy place, and you will see Him clearly.

There is no night in Mary, since there has never been any sin in her, not even the least shadow. She is a holy place. She is the holy of holies, where saints are formed and molded. Note, I pray you, that I say the saints are molded in her.

There is much difference between making a statue with hammer and chisel, hewing it out of wood or stone, and the method of casting in a mold. In the first method the sculptor has much toil. He spends much time, and he may make many blunders. In the second, he works swiftly, without much effort, and without the possibility of marring what he molds.

St. Augustine calls Our Lady "the mold of God." He who is cast into this mold is soon molded into Jesus Christ; and Jesus Christ is molded in him. At little cost, in little time, he will become God! Has he not been cast into the very mold that formed God?

It seems to me I might compare some directors of souls to those sculptors who trust to their own art, ingenuity, or skill. These are the directors wishing to form Christ in themselves or others, but not through true devotion. They strike the hard stone with an infinite number of blows, or dig industriously into some tough block of wood, in an attempt to make an image of Jesus. Frequently they fail to give the image the true look of Jesus. Ignorance or inexperience may be the cause of this. Or a clumsy handling of tools may spoil the whole work—and make all their labor vain.

But those who adopt this secret of grace, this true devotion, this slavery to Jesus in Mary, may rightly be compared to those who use a mold.

Having found the beautiful mold of Mary, where Christ was so naturally and divinely formed, these artists do not need to trust to their own skill or artistry. They trust to the merits of the mold. They throw themselves into it, with those they wish to shape. They lose themselves in it.

They lose themselves in Mary to become true images of her Son!

A beautiful and real simile. But who will understand it? I hope you will.

But remember this. Only what is melted may be cast in a mold. You must melt the old Adam in you to become the new Adam in Mary.

By being perfectly faithful to this devotion, you give more

glory to Christ in a month than you could by any other, even by a harder one, in many years. This is why:

By doing everything through Mary you abandon your own intentions, however good they may be, and lose yourself in those of Mary—though, of course, you cannot know what these are. In this way you participate in the sublimity of her intentions, which are so pure that she gave more glory to God by threading a needle than did St. Lawrence burning to death on his grill, or all the saints in their most heroic deeds. While on earth she attained to such fullness of grace that one could sooner count the stars, or the grains of sand in the desert and on the beaches, or the drops of water in the sea, than the merits that were hers. She gave more glory to God than all the saints and angels have ever given, or will ever give.

Mary, wonder of God! You cannot help but work wonders in the souls who agree to lose themselves in you!

Because by this practice, a soul regards its own thoughts and actions as nothing and relies entirely on the dispositions of Mary—even to speak to her Son—it reaches deeper into the virtue of humility than it would relying on itself. It takes pleasure in this reliance on Mary, not in its own inclinations. Hence it glorifies God in a higher degree. The deeper one's humility, the higher the glory to God. Only the little ones, the humble of heart, truly glorify Him.

Our Lady, because of her great love for us, is eager to receive the gift of our actions. With her immaculate hands she offers them to Jesus, Who is, assuredly, more glorified in this way than He would be if the gift were offered with our own guilty hands.

You never think about Mary without her thinking, in your stead, about God, her Father, Son, and Spouse. You never praise or honor her, without her praising and honoring

God with you. Mary is entirely relative to God. I would even term her the relation to God, for she exists only in relation to Him. She might even be called an echo of the Most High; for she keeps repeating "God . . . God . . . God!" If you say "Mary," she says "God." When Elizabeth praised her, on the occasion of the Visitation, Mary intoned her Magnificat . . . "My soul doth magnify the Lord and my spirit hath rejoiced in God, my Saviour."

What Mary did then she does today. When we praise her, love her, honor her, give anything to her, mention her name with love, God is praised, God is loved, God is honored, we give to God through her and in her.

CHAPTER XV

EXTERIOR PRACTICES

Practices Proper to True Devotion

Although the essence of true devotion lies in the heart, it nevertheless has several exterior practices which one must not neglect. "This must be done, but that must not be omitted." Exterior practices, well performed, help perfect the interior actions. And they remind a man, who is always guided by his senses, of what he has done or has to do. Then too these outward signs of inward devotion help to edify others.

Let no critic thrust his nose into this dissertation to say that one must avoid all that is exterior, that there may be vanity there, or that one should hide his heart's devotion from all others. I answer with my Master: "Let men see your good works that they may glorify your Father Who is in heaven." St. Gregory says, "We do not perform exterior actions and devotions in order to please men, or to win any praises. That would be vanity. But we sometimes perform them in public with the intention of pleasing and glorifying God without any concern for the praises or the scorn of onlookers."

I will mention a few of these exterior practices. I call them exterior because they imply something outside one, not because they are done without an inner spirit. I thus distinguish them from those that are purely inward.

CONSECRATION

Those who wish to adopt this particular devotion—
which has not been established as a confraternity,* although
this is desirable—should first spend at least twelve days
emptying themselves of the spirit of the world, which is contrary to the spirit of Christ. This as a preparation for the reign
of Christ. Then they should spend three weeks being filled
with Jesus through Our Lady. Here is the order they should
keep:

During the first week they will offer all their prayers and
spiritual exercises to God, asking for knowledge of themselves and contrition for their sins. They will do everything
in a spirit of humility. They may, if they wish, meditate on
what I have said about our corrupt nature, and picture themselves as nothing but snails, toads, swine, vipers, or stinking
goats.

Or they can meditate on these three sentences of St.
Bernard:

Think of what you were, a rotting seed.

Think of what you are, a bit of decaying matter.

Think of what you will be; the food of worms.

They will ask Our Lord and His Holy Spirit to enlighten them.

"Lord that I may see," or "Lord that I may know myself," or "Come Holy Ghost."

They will recite every day the Litany of the Holy Ghost,
and the prayer given in the first part of this book. They will

* (Editor's Note: De Montfort's wish has been realized.
The first Confraternity of Mary Queen of All Hearts was
founded in 1899.)

have recourse to Our Lady and will ask her for this great grace which must be the foundation of all others. They will say every day the hymn, "Hail Star of the Sea," and the Litany of Our Lady.

During the second week they will endeavor in all their prayers and daily tasks to know Our Lady. They will ask this knowledge from the Holy Ghost. They may read, and meditate upon, what we have said about her. They will recite, as they did the first week, the Litany of the Holy Ghost, the "Hail, Star of the Sea," and the whole Rosary every day— or at least five decades, a third of the whole, for this intention.

They will devote the third week to the knowledge of Jesus Christ. They may read, and meditate on, what we have said of Him, and recite the prayer of St. Augustine, which is placed toward the beginning of the second part. They may say and repeat with him a hundred times a day "Lord, that I may know Thee," or "Lord, that I may see Who You Are!" They will recite, as they did the previous weeks, the Litany of the Holy Ghost, and the "Hail Star of the Sea," and will add the Litany of the Holy Name of Jesus every day.

After three weeks they will go to Confession and Communion with the intention of giving themselves to Jesus as His slaves of love, through the hands of Mary. After Communion, which they will try to make according to the method given below, they will recite the text of their consecration. (It will be found later on.) They will have to write it, or have it written, unless it is printed; and they will have to sign it the very day they make it.

It will be good if, on that day, they pay some tribute to Jesus and His Mother, either as a penance for past infidelity to the vow of their Baptism, or to proclaim their dependence on the dominion of Jesus and Mary. This tribute will vary according to the devotion and capacity of each one. It may be a fast, an act of mortification, an alms, the lighting of a votive candle. Should they give but a pin in homage, out of a willing heart, it is enough. For Jesus looks only at the heart.

Every year at least, on this same day, they will renew the same consecration, observing the same practices for three weeks. They may renew every month, or every day, all that they have done, by saying these few words:

"I am all Thine, and all I have is Thine, O most lovable Jesus, through Mary, Thy holy mother."

THE LITTLE CROWN

They will recite, every day of their lives, and without compulsion, the Little Crown of Mary, composed of three Our Fathers and twelve Hail Marys, in honor of the twelve privileges and glories of Our Lady. This practice is very old. It has its foundation in Holy Scripture. St. John saw a woman crowned with twelve stars, clothed with the sun, and having the moon beneath her feet. This woman, according to the interpreters, is Our Lady.

There are many ways of saying the Little Crown well, which would take too long to enumerate. The Holy Ghost will teach them to those most faithful to the devotion.

However, in all simplicity, one must first say: "Grant that I may praise thee, Holy Virgin; give me strength against thine enemies." Then one will say the Creed, one Our Father, four Hail Marys, a Glory Be, then another Our Father, another four Hail Marys, a Glory Be, and so on. At the end one says the "We fly to thy patronage, etc. . . ."

THE LITTLE CHAINS

It is most praiseworthy, useful, and glorious, for those who have thus made themselves the slaves of Jesus in Mary to wear a little iron chain, or chains, properly blessed, as a token of their slavery of love.

These exterior marks, to tell the truth, are not essential; and one may certainly do without them, although he has embraced this devotion. Yet I cannot help but praise those who, having shaken off the shameful chains of slavery to the devil, have put on the chains of slavery to Jesus. With St. Paul they glorify themselves by being in chains for the sake of Christ—chains a thousand times more glorious and precious than all the golden necklaces of emperors and queens.

Although in the old days there was nothing more infamous than the cross, today this is by far the most glorious symbol in Christianity. We may say the same of the iron chains of slavery. Nothing was more shameful among the ancients, or is now among the pagans. But among Christians there is nothing more glorious than these chains of Jesus. These fetters have set us free! They guard us from being fettered by the devil. They bind us to Jesus and Mary, not by force but by love. We are not like the galley slaves, chained to hard labor for the rest of our lives. We are like the children of God, who should be drawn "with the bands of love" (Osee, 11, 4).

"I will draw them to me," God says through the mouth of a prophet, "with chains of love," which are as strong as death; and, in a way stronger than death for those who faithfully wear those glorious symbols. Death may destroy and corrupt their bodies but it will not destroy the bonds of their slavery. These, being made of iron, do not easily decay. And it may be that on the day of the resurrection of all flesh, on that great and terrible day of judgment, those chains will shine with glory.

Happy then, unspeakably happy, those slaves of Jesus in Mary who carry their chains into the grave.

Here are the motives for wearing these little chains.

They remind the Christian of the vows and promises of his Baptism, or the perfect renewal of them he made through this devotion, and of the strict obligations he has of being faithful to them. As a man, who directs himself more often through his senses than through pure faith, often forgets his duties to God, these chains may remind him of them. They are also a wonderful help in recollecting that we are no longer slaves of Satan. One of the reasons so few Christians think about their Baptismal vows, and one of the reasons they live with as much license as the pagans, is that they do not wear any exterior symbol to remind them of their promises to God.

These chains show we are not ashamed of our slavery to Jesus, and that we are glad we have renounced the slavery of the world, the flesh and the devil. They prevent us from putting on Satan's chains; for we must, of necessity, wear either the chains of wickedness or of salvation.

Ah, dear brothers and sisters, it is good to break the chains of sin and sinner, the chains of worldlings and of the world, the chains of the devil and his angels. Let us throw the broken yokes, these yokes of death, far from us. Then let us place our feet in the glorious irons of the Holy Ghost, and our necks into His collars. "Yield foot of thine to wisdom's fetters, neck of thine to her collar" (Ecclus. 6, 25). Let us bow our shoulders and carry this wisdom, which is Jesus. Yet let us take no sorrow from His chains. "Yield shoulder of thine to her yoke; do not chafe at her bonds" (Ecclus. 6, 26).

You will note that before saying those words the Holy Ghost prepares the soul so that it may not reject His important counsel. These are His words, "My son, give good heed to the warnings of experience, do not spurn this counsel of mine" (Ecclus. 6, 24).

You are willing, my very dear friends, that I should unite myself to the Holy Ghost and give you the same counsel; "There is life in those trappings, healing virtue in those bonds" (Ecclus. 6, 31).

As Jesus, crucified, must willy-nilly draw all things to Himself, He will draw the wicked by the chains of their sins, and chain them to His everlasting anger and His avenging justice.

And, especially in the latter times, He will draw the chosen, the elect, by the chains of love. "I will draw all things to myself." "They should be drawn with leading-strings of love."

These loving slaves of Jesus, these chained ones of the Lord, may wear their chains either around their necks, or their arms, their waists, or their ankles. Father Vincent Caraffa, the seventh general of the Company of Jesus, who died in 1649 in the odor of sanctity, wore an iron band around one ankle as a token of his slavery. He used to say he was sorry he could not drag his chain in public.

Mother Agnes of Jesus, who has been mentioned before, wore an iron chain around her waist. Others have worn chains about their necks, as a penance for the pearl necklaces they had worn in the world. Some wear the chain around an arm to remind them even while they are at work, that they are slaves of Christ.

DEVOTION TO THE INCARNATION

Slaves of Jesus in Mary will have a special devotion to the great mystery of the Incarnation of the Word, March 25th. This is the mystery proper to true devotion because it has been inspired by the Holy Ghost.

It was inspired that we might see—and honor and imitate—the utter dependence of God on the Virgin Mary for His Father's glory and for our salvation.

This dependence is revealed particularly in this mystery. Jesus, the Son of God, is a captive and slave in the womb of Mary. And He depends upon this humble woman for all things.

We must certainly use this occasion to thank God for the incomparable graces He has granted Mary in choosing her for His Mother—the choice celebrated in this feast day.

These are the two principal ends of the slavery of Jesus Christ in Mary.

Notice, I beg you, that ordinarily I say "slave of Jesus in Mary," or "slavery of Jesus in Mary." One might also, assuredly, say "slave of Mary," or "slavery of Our Lady." I think it better to call oneself the slave of Jesus in Mary, however. Thus, Father Tronson, the superior general of the seminary of St. Sulpice, once advised a cleric who asked his opinion on this subject. Here are the motives:

(1) Since we live in a proud century among a great number of puffed-up scholars, and proud and critical minds, men who find fault with the best established customs of

piety, it is better to say "slavery of Jesus in Mary" and to call oneself a slave of Jesus rather than a slave of Mary— naming the devotion after its Last End, Jesus, and not after the way to arrive at that End, Mary.

Truthfully, though, one may call himself a slave of Mary, even as I do, without scruples. A man going from Orleans to Tours by way of Amboise might well say he was going to Tours, and also that he is going to Amboise. He is a traveller to Amboise and to Tours. Amboise is but a stopping place on the road to Tours. And the road from Amboise to Tours, the last end of the journey, is a straight one.

(2) As the principal mystery celebrated in this devotion is that of the Incarnation—Jesus made flesh in the womb of Mary—it is more fitting we should say "slavery of Jesus in Mary." By this we signify the mystery of Jesus abiding and reigning in Mary. And there is the prayer recited by so many great souls; "O Jesus living in Mary, come and live in us, in Thy spirit of sanctity. . . ."

(3) This way of speaking shows more clearly the intimate union there is between Jesus and Mary. They are so closely united that One is all in the other. Jesus is all in Mary. And Mary is all in Jesus. Rather she is no more, but Jesus alone is in her; and one might sooner separate the light from the sun than Mary from Jesus. So we may call Our Lord "Jesus of Mary," and Our Lady, "Mary of Jesus."

Since time does not permit me to explain here the splendor of the mystery of Jesus living and reigning in Mary, or of the Incarnation of the Word, I will content myself with remarking that this is the first mystery of Jesus, the most hidden, the highest, the most unknown.

It is in this mystery that Jesus, in the womb of Mary, chose all the elect! It is for this reason the saints sometimes refer to the Virgin womb as the "chamber of the secrets of God."

It is in this mystery that Jesus worked all the mysteries of His life. He worked them by accepting them. Therefore this mystery is a summary of all mysteries, and contains the will and the grace of them all.

And this mystery is the throne of the mercy, of the liberality, and of the glory of God. It is the throne of His mercy toward us because one cannot see Jesus, nor speak to Him, nor come near Him, except through the mediation of Mary. Jesus, Who always listens to His Mother, always grants, through her, His grace and His mercy to us sinners. "Let us come boldly, then, before the throne of grace." (Heb. 4, 16.)

It is the throne of His liberality toward Mary because, while this new Adam dwelt here, in His earthly paradise, He secretly worked so many wonders that neither men nor angels could count them. Neither could men or angels understand them. This is why the saints call Mary "the magnificence of God"—as if God showed His magnificence only in Mary. "Here, as nowhere else, our Lord reigns in majesty." (Is. 33, 21.)

It is the throne of His glory for His Father, because it is in Mary that Jesus perfectly soothed His Father, irritated against mankind. It is in Mary He perfectly restored the glory that sin had stolen from Him. It is in Mary that, by sacrificing His will, He gave more glory to His Father than had been rendered by all the sacrifices made under the Old Law. It is in Mary that He offered His Father the first infinite glory given Him by man.

THE HAIL MARY

Slaves of Jesus in Mary will have a great love for the recitation of the Hail Mary, the Angelical Salutation. Few Christians, no matter how enlightened, know the excellence, the merit, and the value of this prayer. Nor are they aware of the necessity of saying it often.

Our Lady had to appear several times to great saints such as St. Dominic, St. John Capistrano, and Blessed Alan de La Rupe, to show them the riches of this prayer. They have written fat books about the wonders and the power of the Hail Mary in the conversion of sinners.

They have loudly proclaimed and publicly preached that since the salvation of the world began with the Hail Mary, the salvation of each one in particular was bound up in the prayer. They have declared it a prayer that caused the dry and barren earth to yield the Fruit of Life. They have said that the same prayer, well said, will make the word of God take root and grow in our souls, and bear that Fruit of Life, Jesus Christ. They have asserted that the Hail Mary is the dew of heaven that waters the earth—the soul—and makes it bear its Fruit in time; and they have declared that a soul not watered by that dew brings forth only weeds, and is in danger of damnation.

Our Lady, says Blessed Alan de la Rupe, in his book about the Rosary, once appeared to him, and addressed him as follows: "Know, my son, and understand, and make it known to all, that it is an almost certain sign of damnation to have a horror of the Hail Mary, or an indifference to it, or to neglect it. It is the prayer that restored the world."

These are most terrible words, which would be hard to believe had we not the guarantee of this holy man, and that of St. Dominic before him, and of several other holy people after him, and with the experience of centuries.

For it is common knowledge that those who bear the mark of eternal doom—the impious, the proud, the worldly, the heretics and atheists—hate and despise the Hail Mary. And also the Rosary.

Heretics still recite the Our Father; but not the Hail Mary. Nor the Rosary. They would rather carry a poisonous snake with them than the Rosary. The proud, even though they be Catholics, are like their father, Lucifer. Either they despise the Hail Mary or look upon it with indifference. And they believe the Rosary is good only to keep silly women busy, or to give the ignorant and illiterate something to do with their hands.

It is common knowledge also that those who show any signs of holiness love the Hail Mary and recite it fondly. The more certainly they belong to God, the more they love this angelic greeting. Our Lady said as much to Blessed Alan, after telling him about the "sign of damnation."

I do not know why this is; but I do know it is true. And I know no better way of learning whether or not a person loves God than to learn first if he loves the Hail Mary, and the Rosary of Hail Marys. One may find it impossible, naturally or supernaturally, to say the words; but he may still love them, and inspire others to recite them.

CHOSEN SOULS, SLAVES OF JESUS IN MARY, know that the Hail Mary is, after the Our Father, the most beautiful of all prayers!

It is the most perfect compliment we can pay to Mary, since it is the compliment God paid her, through His archangel. He sent this shining messenger, Gabriel, to win her heart. And Gabriel's greeting so moved that beautiful heart, through the secrets it contains, that Mary, in spite of her humility, consented to become the Mother of God.

By this compliment you also, my dear friends, will win Mary's heart. This without fail, provided you say it properly.

The Hail Mary, said with attention, devotion, and modesty, is the enemy of the devil. It puts the lord of hell to flight. It is the hammer which crushes him. It is the sanctification of souls, the joy of angels, the melodious lyric of the chosen ones, the canticle of the New Testament, the bliss of Mary, and the glory of the Holy Trinity.

The Hail Mary is that dew from heaven that brings fruit to the field of the soul. It is a chaste and loving kiss. It is a crimson rose, a lustrous pearl one offers Mary. It is a mixture of ambrosia and nectar one gives her to drink.

All those comparisons are from the saints.

I beg you, therefore, by the love I bear you in Jesus and Mary, not to be satisfied with a minimum of Hail Marys. Recite the Little Crown of Our Lady, but say your Rosary too—the fifteen decades. Say it every day. And at the hour of your death you will bless the hour you accepted my advice.

If you have sown the blessings of Jesus and Mary in your soul—"blessed art thou among women, and blessed is the fruit of thy womb, Jesus"—you will reap eternal blessings in heaven. "He who sows bountifully will also reap bountifully." (2 Cor. 9, 6.)

SIXTH PRACTICE

In order to thank God for the graces He has bestowed upon Our Lady, the slaves of Jesus in Mary will often recite the *Magnificat*. It is the only prayer Our Lady ever composed. Rather it may be said that Christ composed it in her, for He spoke through her lips. It is the greatest offering of praise God ever received in the order of grace. It is the humblest and most thankful, and it is the most sublime of all canticles. There are so many great and hidden mysteries in it that even the angels do not know them all.

Gerson, a holy and learned doctor of the Church, after he had spent most of his life writing about the most profound subjects, undertook to explain the *Magnificat;* but in fear and trembling. He did this toward the end of his career, wishing thus to crown all his other works. He tells us many marvelous things about this divine and lovely canticle. Our Lady, he says, often recited it herself, especially as a thanksgiving after Holy Communion!

The wise Benzonius, explaining the *Magnificat,* tells of miracles worked through its power. He says the devils flee when they hear the words, "He hath wrought mightily with His arm: He hath scattered the proud in the conceit of their hearts."

SEVENTH PRACTICE

The faithful slaves of Mary must greatly despise and hate this corrupted world, and must flee away from its influences. They must make use of the practices we have given in the first part of this book to strengthen their contempt of the world.

CHAPTER XVI

INTERIOR PRACTICES FOR THOSE WHO WISH TO BECOME PERFECT

Outside of the exterior practices mentioned, which must not be omitted through negligence or contempt, here are some most sanctifying interior practices. They are meant for those whom the Holy Ghost calls to a high perfection.

It is to do all one's actions *by* Mary, *with* Mary, *in* Mary, and *for* Mary, so as to do them more perfectly *by* Jesus, *with* Jesus, *in* Jesus, and *for* Jesus.

BY MARY

They must do all their actions *by* Mary. That is, they must obey Our Lady in all things, and act in all things by her spirit, which is the Holy Spirit of God. "Those who are led by the Spirit of God are children of God." (Rom. 8, 4.)

Those led by the Spirit of Mary are children of Mary, and therefore children of God, as we have shown before. And, among so many devoted to Mary, none are her true and faithful devotees but those who act by her spirit.

I said the spirit of Mary is the Spirit of God because she never acted by her own spirit but always by the Spirit of God. He made Himself master over her to such an extent that He became her own spirit. This is the reason why St. Ambrose says: "May the soul of Mary be in each one, to glorify the Lord. May the spirit of Mary be in each to rejoice in God."

How happy the soul who, after the example of St. Alphonsus Rodriguez, the Jesuit lay brother, is possessed and governed by the spirit of Mary—a spirit meek and strong, zealous and prudent, humble and courageous, pure and fruitful!

In order that the soul may allow itself to be led by this spirit of Mary, one must . . .

First, renounce his own spirit, his own ambitions and ideas. This he must do before he does anything else, before mental prayer, before hearing or saying Mass, before going to Communion . . . because the darkness of one's spirit and the malice of the will, would, if he followed his own inclinations, oppose the holy spirit of Mary. What one had in mind might appear good to him—but he could be mistaken.

Second, one must deliver himself to the spirit of Mary, to be moved and led the way Mary desires. One must place oneself in her possession, and leave himself there, to be used as a tool or an instrument in the hands of a worker, or a lute in the hands of a good musician.

One must abandon himself in her, like a stone that is cast into the sea. This is done simply, in a moment, by a single act of the mind, a small exertion of the will, by a few words—"I give myself to you, Mary, Mother of God, my mother."

One may not feel any happiness in this act of union. But it is none the less a real act of union. It is as real as if one were to say . . . God forbid . . . "I give myself to the devil." Although one might say this, and feel no inward change whatsoever, he would truly belong to the devil.

Third, one must, from time to time, renew the act of offering, and the act of union.

The oftener you do this the sooner you will become a saint. The more you repeat it the sooner you will arrive at union with Jesus, which always, necessarily, follows union with Mary—since the spirit of Mary is the Spirit of Jesus.

WITH MARY

One must do everything *with* Mary. That is we must try to imitate, in our own human way, all the virtues—the perfection—the Holy Ghost fashioned in her.

We must, in each action, consider how Mary did this or that, or how she would do it in our circumstances. Hence we must examine the virtues she practiced, and meditate on them. Particularly we must concern ourself with her lively faith, which made her believe the words of the angel, without the least hesitation; with her deep humility, which made her hide herself, be silent, submit to everything, and put herself in the last place; and with her truly divine purity which never had its equal and never will this side of heaven!

Here I must cry out again that Mary is the unique mold of God, most suitable to produce living images of God at little cost and in little time! A soul who has found this mold, and loses himself in it, is soon transformed into Jesus Christ, Whom this mold perfectly represents.

IN MARY

One must do everything *in* Mary.

To understand this, we must realize that Mary is the true paradise of the new Adam. The Eden from which the old Adam was expelled prefigured her. Our paradise is filled with untold riches, with beauty, with delights, with all sorts of good things that the new Adam left there. He occupied this paradise for nine months, and was well pleased with it. He worked His wonders there. He displayed there His riches, and with divine magnificence.

In this Eden, this weedless garden made fertile by the power of the Holy Ghost, its Tenant, one may find trees which were planted by God and sustained by His grace. There is the tree of life, which bore Jesus as its Fruit. And there is the tree of the knowledge of good and evil, whose fruit was Incarnate Wisdom, the Light of the world.

There are, in this most beautiful place, flowers of various kinds, flowers of virtue, whose fragrance thrills even the angels. There are fields of flowers there, meadows of hope, towers of strength, and mansions of simplicity and trust.

Only the Holy Ghost can make you understand the truth that lies behind these images.

The air is pure. It is the air of purity. Day reigns here. Day without night. A beautiful day, the day of the Sacred Humanity. The sun does not cast a shadow. It is the sun of the Divinity. It is a sun that melts base metals and changes them to gold. A clear spring, humility, here turns itself into four streams—the cardinal virtues—and waters the entire oasis.

The Holy Ghost, speaking through the ancient Fathers of the Church, refers to this garden as the eastern gate through which the High Priest, Jesus, entered the world.

There He came the first time. There He will come once more.

The Holy Spirit also speaks of Mary as the sanctuary of the Divinity, the resting place of the Trinity, the throne of God, the city of God, the altar of God, the temple of God, and the world of God.

What a privilege, what a glory, what a joy, what a rich blessing to be able to enter this new Garden of Eden—to dwell in Mary, where the Most High has placed His throne!

But how difficult it is for sinners like us to obtain the right to venture into a place so holy—and power and intelligence enough to use that right. This paradise is guarded not by a cherub, but by the Holy Ghost Himself. He wields absolute dominion over it. Mary is His closed garden.

"A garden enclosed is my sister, my spouse; a spring shut up; a fountain sealed."

Mary is enclosed. Mary is sealed. The miserable children of Adam and Eve, driven out of the old paradise, cannot enter this one except through permission of the Holy Ghost, a very special grace, which they must earn.

When one has succeeded, through his faithfulness, in obtaining this permission, this grace beyond compare, he must remain in the garden, in happiness, in peace, in trust, and in complete assurance. He must here abandon himself without reserve.

In the fair interior of Mary the soul will be fed on the milk of her grace and mercy. It will be freed from all its anxieties, fears, and scruples; it will be held safe from its enemies, the world, the devil, and the flesh. These enemies never had any entrance here. That is why Mary says that those who work in her will not sin. "He who lives by me will do no wrong." (Eccl. 24, 30.) Those who dwell in Our Lady in spirit will not commit any grievous sin.

In Mary the soul may be formed in Jesus, and Jesus in the soul. Her womb is, as the ancient Fathers say, the chamber of the sacraments of God, where Christ and all the elect were formed.

FOR MARY

And we must do everything *for* Mary. Inasmuch as one has given himself to her, it is right that he should do everything for her, as a servant and a slave. One does not, of course, regard her as the last end of his services—that end is

Christ alone—but as a means to reach that end. As a good servant and slave one must not remain idle.

Depending on the protection of his august sovereign Lady —he must dare and do great things for her. He must defend her rights when they are disputed, and fight for her glory when it is assailed. He must attract the whole world to her service, if he can. He must lift his voice to denounce those who abuse her and outrage her Son. He must do everything in his power to spread true devotion.

And he must ask nothing of her, as a reward for what little he accomplishes, except the honor of belonging absolutely to her; and the joy of being united by her to Jesus, never to be separated from Him.

GLORY TO JESUS IN MARY!
GLORY TO MARY IN JESUS!
GLORY TO GOD ALONE!

CHAPTER XVII

APPLYING TRUE DEVOTION

How To Practice True Devotion in Holy Communion

Before Communion you must (a) humble yourself profoundly before God; (b) renounce your corrupted nature and your dispositions, however good your self-love makes them seem; (c) renew your consecration, saying: "I am all Thine, and all I have is Thine, Lord Jesus, through Mary, Thy holy Mother"; (d) ask Mary to lend you her heart that you may receive Jesus there, and with her dispositions. Tell her the glory of her Son is at stake. He should not be placed in so corrupt and inconsistent a heart as yours. It might lessen His glory, or even destroy it. Tell her that, because of the dominion she has over the hearts of men, she can come into your heart—such as it is—and receive Jesus there. Then there will be no danger of His being unworthily received.

Tell her that all you have given her is nothing, but that now, through Holy Communion you wish to give her the same present God the Father gave her!

Tell her that Jesus, Who loves her with a divine love, a unique love, still desires to rest and delight in her, although He must come to your soul to do so . . . a soul filthier and poorer than the stable in which He was born, the mean little stable He loved because Mary was there.

And implore her to give you her heart, using these tender words: "I receive you as my all; give me your heart."

IN COMMUNION:

When you are about to receive Jesus Christ, after the

123

Our Father in the Mass, say three times, "Lord, I am not worthy."

Speak to the Father. Tell Him you are unworthy to receive His only begotten Son because of your evil thoughts and your ingratitude. But remind Him of Mary—"Behold the handmaid of the Lord." She will act in your stead, and give you confidence and hope before His Majesty. "What need, O Lord, of aught but Thyself, to bring me confidence?"

Speak to God the Son. "Lord I am not worthy." Tell Him you are unworthy to receive Him because of your evil and idle words and your faithlessness in His service. Ask His mercy, that you may bring Him into the house of His Mother, and yours.

Tell Him you will not let Him go until He comes to dwell in her home. "I will never leave him, never let him go, till I have brought him in my own mother's house, into the room that saw my birth." (Canticle of Sol. 3, 4.)

Beg Him to come into the place of His rest, the ark of His glory. "Up, Lord, and take possession of thy resting-place; thou and the ark that is thy shrine." (Ps. 131, 9.)

Tell Him you have no confidence in your own merits, as Esau did, but that you rely on the virtues of your mother, as Jacob did. Sinner that you are, you dare approach His holiness only because of the merits of His Mother, Mary. Tell Him that.

Speak to the Holy Ghost. "Lord I am not worthy." Tell Him you are unworthy to receive the masterpiece of His love because of your lukewarmness, the wickedness of your conduct, and your opposition to His inspirations. But tell Him all your trust is in His faithful spouse, Mary. Say with St. Bernard, "She is my greatest confidence. She is the whole reason of my hope." Beg Him to come once more to Mary.

Her womb is as pure and her heart as ardent as ever. Tell Him too that if He does not also enter your poor soul, neither Mary nor Jesus will find it a worthy dwelling.

AFTER COMMUNION.

Recollect yourself. Close your eyes. Introduce Jesus into the heart of Mary. Give Him to His Mother. She will greet Him with love and adoration. She will embrace Him. She will give Him the place of honor and do a million things for Him unknown to you in your most extreme darkness.

Keep humble in the presence of Jesus living in Mary. Fancy yourself a slave waiting at the gate of the royal palace while the King of Kings is speaking to the Queen. While they take delight in each other—without any need of you— go in spirit through heaven and earth, asking all creatures to thank, adore, and love Jesus in Mary for you. "O come let us adore Him—Christ, the King!"

Or pray to Jesus in union with Mary. Ask for the coming of His kingdom on earth, through His Mother. Beg for divine wisdom, for divine love, for the forgiveness of your sins, or for some particular grace you need. But always *by* Mary and *in* Mary.

Look down upon yourself and say: "Lord do not look at my sins" . . . let Your eyes see nothing but the virtues and the merits of Mary."

At the remembrance of your sins, say, "An enemy has done this." You, your own worst enemy, have committed those sins. Or say, "Deliver me from the unjust and deceitful man" . . . (Ps. 42, 1) or, "He must increase and I must decrease" (John 3, 30) . . . "Jesus, You must increase in my heart and I must decrease: Mary, you must increase in me and I become less than I was" . . . or "Increase and multiply"

. . . Gen. 1, 22) . . . "O Jesus and Mary, increase in me, and multiply Yourselves in others."

There are a thousand other thoughts that the Holy Spirit inspires. He will teach you them if you are really spiritual, mortified, and true to this great true devotion.

Remember, the more you let Mary act in your Communion, the more you will glorify Jesus. The way to let Mary act for Jesus, and Jesus act in Mary, is to humble yourself as much as you can, without trying to see or taste or feel. The just man lives by faith, everywhere; but particularly in Holy Communion. "The just man liveth by faith" (Heb. 10, 38).

APPENDIX I

CONSECRATION TO JESUS CHRIST, THE INCARNATE WISDOM, THROUGH THE HANDS OF MARY

O eternal, incarnate Wisdom, lovable, adorable Jesus, only begotten Son of the Father and of Mary ever Virgin, I adore You profoundly in the bosom and the splendor of Your Father, in eternity, and in the virgin womb of Mary during the time of Your Incarnation.

I give You thanks for annihilating Yourself and taking the form of a slave to set me free from the cruel slavery of the devil. I give You thanks, and I glorify You, because You consented to submit to Mary in all things, in order to make me Your faithful slave through her.

Alas, ungrateful and unfaithful, I did not keep the solemn promises of my Baptism. I did not fulfill my obligations. I do not deserve to be called either Your child or Your slave. And since there is nothing in me that does not deserve Your hostility and anger, I dare not come alone to Your august and holy presence.

That is why I have recourse to the intercession of Your Mother, whom You gave me as a mediatrix with You. It is through her I hope to obtain from You contrition for my sins and forgiveness of them; and to be given Your wisdom, that I may keep it.

Hail Mary immaculate, living tabernacle of God! Hidden in you, Eternal Wisdom wants to be adored by men and angels.

Hail Queen of heaven and earth. To you all things are subject; all things that are under God.

Hail sure refuge of sinners, whose mercy has failed no one. Grant my desire for divine Wisdom, and receive the vows and offerings my lowliness therefore presents you.

I . . . a faithless sinner, renew and ratify today in your hands, O immaculate mother, the vows of my Baptism. I renounce forever Satan, his pomps and works; and I give myself entirely to Jesus Christ, the Incarnate Wisdom, to carry my cross after Him all the days of my life, and to be more faithful to Him than I have ever been before.

In the presence of all the court of heaven, I choose you this day for my mother and mistress. I deliver and consecrate to you, as your slave, my body and soul, my goods, both interior and exterior, and even the value of all my good actions, past, present, and future; leaving to you the entire and full right of disposing of me and all that belongs to me, without exception, according to your good pleasure, for the greater glory of God, in time and in eternity.

Receive, O merciful Virgin, this little offering of my slavery. I wish thereby to pay homage to Jesus, and unite myself to Him Who willed to be subjected to your maternity; and to pay homage to the power You both have over this little worm, this miserable sinner, and in thanksgiving for the privileges with which the Holy Trinity has favored thee.

I declare that I want, now, as your slave, to seek your honor and to obey you in all things.

Admirable mother, present me to your Son, as His slave forever, so that, inasmuch as He has redeemed me by you, He may receive me by you.

O mother of mercy, grant me the grace to obtain the true Wisdom of God and to be placed, for that end, among those you love, those you teach, those you direct, those you nourish and protect as your children and slaves.

Faithful Virgin, make me in all things so perfect a disciple, slave, and imitator of Jesus, your Son, Incarnate Wisdom, that I may, through you and after your example, come to the fullness of His age on earth and of His glory in heaven. Amen.

APPENDIX II

PRAYER TO JESUS

Jesus, my love, my God, let me speak to You. Let me thank You for giving me to Mary as her slave. You gave her to me as my advocate with You and my universal support in my extreme misery. My misery is great. Alas, Lord, I am such a wretch that I would be lost without her. I need her. I need her with You. I need her at all times. I need her to avert Your anger from me, for I offend You every day. I need her to fend off the punishments I deserve from You. I need her to look at You, to speak to You, to pray to You, to go to You, to please You. I need her to save my soul. Mine and others. I need her to do Your will and seek Your glory in all things.

Ah, if I could only tell the whole universe about Your mercy to me! If I could only let the world know how lost I should be without Mary! If only I could thank You properly for so divine a blessing!

Mary is in me. Mary was made for me. She is my treasure, my comfort. Can I not be all hers? O my Saviour, how awful if I could not! Rather let me die than suffer such misfortune. I would rather not live than not belong entirely to her.

Like St. John at the foot of the cross I have taken her for my own. Thousands of times. And thousands of times I have given her myself. If I have not yet done it as You require, Jesus, let me do it now. If You see in me, body and soul, anything that does not belong to her, my queen, take it out and dispose of it. If it is not Mary's it is not worthy of You.

Holy Ghost, plant, tend, and nourish in me the Tree of Life, Your pure love, Mary. Make it blossom and bear the Fruit of Life. Give me a great devotion to Mary, so that, in her, I may be made into the perfect likeness of Jesus, in all His stature and might, unto the fullness of his age. Amen.

APPENDIX III

PRAYER TO MARY

Hail Mary, beloved daughter of the Father, admirable Mother of the Son, faithful spouse of the Holy Ghost! Hail Mary, my dear mother, my sweet mistress, my powerful queen. Hail, my joy, my glory, my heart, my soul. You are all mine, by mercy; and I am all yours, by justice. But not enough.

I give myself to you once again, as your slave forever. I do not keep anything, either for myself or others. If you still see in me something that does not belong to you, please take it away this very moment. Make yourself absolute mistress over me. Destroy, uproot, and annihilate in me all that displeases God. And plant and nurture and raise in me all you will.

May the light of your faith dispel the darkness in my mind. May your profound humility take the place of my pride. May your lofty contemplation put an end to the distractions of my wandering imagination. May your constant sight of God fill my memory with His presence. May the fire of love in your heart expand and kindle the lukewarmness and the coldness in mine. May your virtues replace my sins. May your merits be my ornament and my unmerited bounty before God.

My dear and much loved mother, let me have no other mind than yours to know your Son and His divine will, no other soul than yours with which to praise and glorify Him, no other heart than yours with which to love Him.

I do not ask for visions, for revelations, for spiritual favors of any sort. To see clearly without darkness is yours. To enjoy fully, and without bitterness, is yours. To triumph gloriously in heaven at the right hand of the Lord, is yours. Absolute sway over men and angels is yours; and dominion over the devil and all his armies. All the good things of God are yours without reserve, to dispose of as you will.

This, O holy Virgin, the Most High has already given you. It shall not be taken from you. That is my joy. As for my lot in life, I want only what was yours—to believe by pure faith and without the help of my senses; to suffer joyfully and without consolation all that is alloted me to suffer; to die continually to self, without relaxing; and to work industriously and exceedingly well for you, without reward, as the lowest of your slaves, until I die.

I ask of your pure mercy this grace only—that I may always say, "Amen, so be it," to all you are doing on earth; to all you do in heaven; and to all you can do in my soul.

May you be all alone in me to give full glory to Jesus, in time and in eternity!

Amen; so be it!

APPENDIX IV

THE CONFRATERNITY OF MARY
QUEEN OF ALL HEARTS

ORIGIN: The Confraternity was first established in Canada, by Archbishop Duhamel of Ottawa, on March 25th. 1899. On April 28th. 1913 it was canonically erected as an Archconfraternity in Rome. Many centres have since been established in different countries.

OBJECT: The object of the confraternity is to establish within us the Reign of Mary as a means of establishing more perfectly the Reign of Jesus Christ in our souls.

CONDITIONS OF MEMBERSHIP:

1. To send in your name to be recorded in the official Register by the Father Director, who will send you a certificate of membership.

2. To prepare yourself to make the Act of Consecration to Jesus by the hands of Mary on a special day, preferably a feastday of Our Lady.

3. To perform a good work in honour of our Lady on the day of consecration.

4. *(optional)* To wear the badge of Confraternity, which is a medal of our Lady, Queen of our hearts; but this is not required of those who wear a crucifix in some visible way.

PRACTICES:

To renew every morning the act of consecration to Jesus through Mary, at least by using the following formula: *'I belong wholly to you and all that I have I offer you, O most loving Jesus, through Mary, your holy Mother.'*

They should apply themselves to live always in dependence on Mary and to do all their actions in union with her.

INDULGENCES

On the occasion of the initial consecration (using the De Montfort formula) or, on the occasion of its renewal, a PLENARY INDULGENCE is granted, under the usual conditions (Confession, Communion and prayer for the intentions of the Holy Father). Also, a PLENARY INDULGENCE on the following days: 1 – The day of enrollment in the Confraternity; 2 – Holy Thursday; 3 – Christmas; 4 – Feast of the Annunciation; 5 – Feast of the Immaculate Conception (Dec. 8); 6 – St. Louis de Montfort's Feast day (April 28); 7 – Every First Saturday of the Month.

In answer to a petition by the Montfort Missionaries to the Sacred Penitentiary in Rome, the above indulgences were granted for a period of 10 years (as of Oct. 10, 1986), to the two Confraternities (Priests of Mary, Queen of All Hearts and the Confraternity of Mary, Queen of All Hearts), thus bringing them in line with the conditions laid down in the new ENCHIRIDION of Indulgences.

All members share in the merits and prayers and good works of both congregations founded by St. Louis Marie. For further information one should write to:

Reverend Father Director,
The Confraternity,
26 So. Saxon Ave.
Bay Shore, N.Y. 11706

MONTFORTIAN CONGREGATIONS

St. Louis Marie de Montfort founded two religious Congregations: The Company of Mary (Montfort Missionaries) and the Daughters of Wisdom (Montfort Sisters). Both Congregations aspire to live the spirituality of their holy Founder, especially his devotion to our Lady, as set forth in "True Devotion to the Blessed Virgin," and to spread this devotion through their apostolic work.

MONTFORT MISSIONARIES: This Congregation is made up of priests and brothers who devote themselves to missionary work at home and abroad. The members number about 1,200. The missionary field comprises France, Canada, Spain, U.S.A., Australia, England, Ireland, Scotland, Holland, Italy, Portugal, Columbia, Haiti, Malawi, Zaire, Madagascar, Papua, Iceland, Nicaragua and others.

Young men aspiring to the missionary vocation should apply to:

> The Director of
>   Vocations,
> Montfort Missionaries,
> 101-18, 104 St.
> Ozone Park, N.Y. 11416

MONTFORT SISTERS: The congregation numbers about 4,500 sisters who devote themselves to the education of youth, the nursing of the sick and handicapped and apostolic work on the Foreign Missions. Young ladies who wish to enter the Congregation should apply to:

> Reverend Mother Provincial,
> 385 Ocean Ave.
> Islip, N.Y. 11751

Once called "America's Star Reporter" Eddie Doherty was a newspaperman for over thirty years. He has written for many large dailies, was City Editor of the *New York America* and staff-writer for a popular national magazine. In 1943 he married Baroness Catherine de Hueck, founder of Friendship House. In recent years Eddie has dedicated his pen almost exclusively to religious themes. On August 15, 1969, at the age of 79, Eddie Doherty was ordained a priest in the Melkite rite. He died May 4, 1975.